HOMOSEXUALITY

Christian truth and love

EDITOR: PAUL E BROWN

DayOne

© Day One Publications 2007
First printed 1998, revised 2007

ISBN 978-1-84625-054-5

ISBN 978-1-84625-054-5

British Library Cataloguing in Publication Data available

Published by Day One Publications
Ryelands Road, Leominster, HR6 8NZ
☎ 01568 613 740 FAX 01568 611 473
email—sales@dayone.co.uk
web site—www.dayone.co.uk
North American—e-mail—sales@dayonebookstore.com
North American—web site—www.dayonebookstore.com

Designed by Steve Devane and printed by Gutenberg Press, Malta

Contents

Preface

In 1998 Day One produced *Homosexuality: the straight agenda* in the series 'Facing the issue', a series sponsored by the Theological Committee of the Fellowship of Independent Evangelical Churches. But things have changed over the past eight years. The Theological Committee has moved from FIEC to come under the umbrella of Affinity. The original series of books was completed and no new ones are foreseen. The cultural outlook and legislation concerning homosexuals have also markedly changed. This book is more than a revision of the previous one. The Introduction and two chapters are entirely new; some chapters in the older book no longer appear, and the chapters that remain have been revised, some quite extensively. But the issue itself is more pressing than ever, and the situation increasingly more difficult for those who believe—as Brian Edwards put it in the previous book—'that the teaching of the Bible is decisive on all matters of morality and ... that, on this matter, its teaching is unequivocally straightforward'.

Paul E. Brown

List of contributors

PAUL E. BROWN is a retired pastor.

REV. DR KENNETH BROWNELL is the pastor of East London Tabernacle Baptist Church and editor of the theological journal Foundations.

DECLAN FLANAGAN is the chief executive of Rural Ministries.

MARTIN HALLETT is the director of True freedom Trust, a Christian support and teaching ministry offering hope and help to men and women struggling with homosexuality, lesbianism and similar issues, and to their families and friends.

ROGER HITCHINGS is the pastor of East Leake Evangelical Church.

DR PETER SAUNDERS is the general secretary of the Christian Medical Fellowship.

The message which Christian churches are to proclaim has these two defining characteristics. Firstly, it is a good message, one that promises good things for those who receive it. This is what is meant by the word 'gospel'. In the unforgettable words of William Tyndale, the Bible translator, 'This ... signifieth good, merry, glad and joyful tidings, that maketh a man's heart glad, and maketh him sing, dance and leap for joy.' Secondly, it is a message for every person without exception. It is for 'all the people' (Luke 2:10), for everyone from every part of the world, whoever they are, whatever their character and whatever their behaviour; the good, the bad and the ugly!

These two characteristics are absolutely fundamental. The Christian message is for all and it holds out what is good for all. It is not a message that leads to restriction and slavery, but to peace and love. It aims to set people free, to bring them joy and happiness, to fill them with hope, to transform life now, and to hold out the promise of something far better in a life beyond this one. It offers a fullness of life that cannot be found or known from anywhere else. It is a message which comes from God and which leads to him: 'This is eternal life, that they know you the only true God, and Jesus Christ whom you have sent' (John 17:3). The churches have been entrusted with this message and it is their responsibility to tell it faithfully to everyone. No one is excluded. All who receive and believe the message will know God, receive eternal life and become his children: 'To all who did receive him, who believed in his name, he gave the right to become children of God' (John 1:12).

It is important to state this straight away. This book is a discussion of sexual behaviour from a Christian perspective, but a Christian perspective means it comes in the context of the message that has been described. Nothing would bring more joy to those who contributed to this book than to find that some who read it are led to consider seriously the Christian gospel and in so doing come to Jesus Christ himself.

This message is for all because everyone needs it. It is addressed to those who have fallen short of God's standards of behaviour, something true of everyone. It is a message of forgiveness and restoration for those who have fallen. It is a good message because it promises hope and a new start to those who need it. No one denies the distinction between right and wrong.

Introduction

Everyone accepts that there is much that is wrong about their own lives and the lives of everyone else they know. The Christian message necessarily comes in the context of God's assessment of right and wrong.

This relates to the gospel message in two ways. Firstly, the gospel is a message that tells how we can be right with God. It tells how human sin can be forgiven so that we can have fellowship with a God of perfect holiness. However, until someone comes to realise a need for forgiveness, until people become aware that they are far from God and need to be brought back to him, they will not seek for this. Becoming convinced of one's own sin, at least in some measure, is a necessity for reception of the gospel and trust in Jesus Christ. So those who preach the gospel also need to point out to their hearers the sinful and estranged condition that they are in. As Jesus said, 'It is not the healthy who need a doctor, but the sick. I have not come to call the righteous, but sinners to repentance' (Luke 5:31–32, NIV).

Secondly, those who believe in Jesus Christ begin a new life. That life is one of joy and fellowship with God, but also includes living by God's standards. While no Christian reaches those standards fully, that is what we desire, and that is what we aim at. It is part of the honesty of preaching the gospel that those who hear are left in no doubt that turning to the Lord involves a life of obedience to the standards set out in the Bible. It is right that potential disciples, as well as actual disciples, should understand what it means to be a follower of Christ.

This might seem to strike a somewhat negative note, so two further points can be added. The Christian life is actually a life that is good, satisfying and joyful. It is demanding, in that it calls for sacrifice, self-denial and obedience, yet it is also glorious. It is life with Jesus Christ. It is a life lived in the power of the Holy Spirit. It is a life lived in fellowship with other believers in the church. Even when there are persecutions and hardships it is the best life of all. It is the nearest to human experience as it was intended to be that we can reach in the present world. Moreover—and here is the second point—it is life that never ends but which opens out after our life in this world. For the Christian, to die is to be with Christ, which is far better than anything possible here. Then, after the resurrection, there will be a life that goes far beyond our wildest imaginations now. Whatever hardships and difficulties may come our way in the present, the prospect that the Bible sets before us is one that far outweighs anything we may experience now: 'For this slight momentary affliction is preparing for us an eternal weight of glory beyond all comparison' (2 Corinthians 4:17).

Some people might be tempted to think all this is merely a softening-up process leading to a condemnation of homosexuals and homosexuality. Rather, it is a necessary explanatory introduction. If you attend service twice a Sunday in evangelical churches you are likely to hear the gospel message frequently, but you might go for years without hearing homosexuality mentioned at all. The Bible has just eight passages in which it is generally believed homosexual conduct is referred to. These passages are carefully examined later, and it is right to say now that they contain explicit prohibition of such behaviour. However, there are some fourteen or fifteen times as many references to fornication and adultery, which are similarly prohibited, and sins like pride, greed, lying, hypocrisy, stealing and idolatry are often strongly condemned. All have sinned and the message that the churches have for homosexual people is the same message that it has for everyone else. It is the gospel message of forgiveness of sins—all and every kind of sin—and of new life, of service for God and fulfilment in doing his will.

We live in days of gross sexual immorality. Fornication and adultery are commonplace, pornography is readily available and pornographic images seep into many magazines, papers and advertising. All this is looked on as up-to-date and liberating. It is, of course, simply a reversion to pagan immoralism, though presented in a modern sophisticated dress with modern justifications. It is surely true to say that a section of this is gay, lesbian and bisexual. To many this section appears to be the public face of the homosexual scene: Gay Pride marches and celebrations, gay night-clubs, bath-houses and pubs, soliciting in public toilets and so on. It is arguable that this should be looked on as just one part of a wider scene of rampantly irresponsible and humanly damaging sexual behaviour that undermines marriage and family life, breaks with the mores of many cultures, and seriously violates God's laws.

But not all homosexuals, by any means, are satisfied with that scene or belong to it. There are those who are looking for love and companionship, a relationship that is stable and committed, a sexual relationship which, because they find no attraction in the opposite sex, they look for with someone of the same sex. This is a different outlook from the free-wheeling, free-for-all attitude of the promiscuous, whether homosexual or heterosexual. This is the only kind of sexual relationship that those who take a 'gay Christian' approach could possibly argue for. This is not something that the Bible allows, so this book contends, but we ought to distinguish those who adopt this approach from the former.

There are also many people who believe that sexual relations belong within marriage, who accept that and desire to live accordingly, but being single find themselves sorely tried and tempted, and perhaps sometimes fall. In this category there are almost certainly more heterosexuals than homosexuals. It is probable that this group of people is wider than we sometimes imagine and goes considerably further than the bounds of evangelical Christianity. We might also remember that there are people who have a wide variety of sexual fantasies and fetishes. There are not a few people who indulge, at least occasionally, in practices which they feel impelled towards and yet which afterwards leave them feeling ashamed, sometimes filled with self-loathing, even self-hatred. In most cases these are people who know they need help but are afraid and ashamed to ask for it. We need to have some understanding of the wide variety of outlook and attitude to be met with today, though these paragraphs necessarily express very broad generalisations.

How is it that our culture has reached its present state? Nowadays the legitimacy of homosexual relationships is often taught in schools and is widely accepted. Civil partnerships between homosexuals are very similar to marriage in a number of respects. We live in a society that, in general terms, does not accept standards that are derived from the Bible. This is the case even with some people who claim to be Christian. This book will argue that there is no valid case for believing that the Bible justifies homosexual behaviour or that its prohibitions are irrelevant to our modern situation, but the current position makes it very difficult for young people growing up in Bible-based churches, and for evangelising a society based on secularism and relativism. What are some of the reasons for the change of climate that has taken place in our society over the past forty years or so?

First of all there is now a different way of looking at sexuality and sex.

Because of the widespread availability of contraceptives, intercourse has become divorced from procreation in the minds of most people. Procreation is an option, but that is all it is. And because sex is fun and good for you (at least in the sense that it removes sexual tension—in the short term), people are now free to indulge in sexual behaviour if they wish, and many do.

It is also now possible to have a baby by means other than simple intercourse between a man and a woman. Egg donation, sperm donation and surrogacy are present options, and cloning a possible future option, as well as the possibility that stem cells may be able to be developed into sperm or ova. Homosexual couples can have children by these methods as well as heterosexuals. Adoption is also now an option for homosexual couples. It is no longer necessary to have a heterosexual relationship, however brief, in order to have a child. There is little doubt that marriage in its traditional sense has been devalued.

Another reason for the change is revulsion at past prejudice towards homosexuals and the discriminatory attitude that goes with it. Actual violence to homosexuals, as well as verbal abuse, has been far too prevalent and is by no means simply a thing of the past. Unfortunately Christian attitudes have sometimes reinforced the aggressive posture that some have taken to homosexuals, though this has generally been quite unintentional. There is a strong anti-discriminatory feeling in today's society from which homosexuals have benefited.

There is also the current stress on individual human rights. Western society is strongly individualistic and people are quick to assert their 'rights' as they see them. This goes beyond homosexuality, of course, but it is easy to see how homosexuals can claim it as their right to live in accord with their own sexuality, and reject the right of others to impose what they consider alien values on them.

Both of these last two reasons are closely related to today's emphasis on tolerance. Tolerance is the great virtue. People have different ideas and different lifestyles and we must all tolerate each other, so it is said. It is a difficult area, for we believe in tolerance too, but it is the tolerance of love, rather than a love of tolerance. The tolerance that springs from love wants to win over rather than compel. God tolerates the unbelief and disobedience of people, but he sends his messengers among them to tell his gospel. They go to win people by the truth of what they say and by the holiness and love that their lives display.

A further reason is the widespread belief that one's sexuality is fixed. Homosexuals, it is said, are not heterosexuals who simply want to be different, they are not deliberately deviant, they were born that way. Although this is a widespread perception, it is by no means as simple as that. Some heterosexuals do appear to pass through a homosexual phase, or at least a phase when they are unsure of their sexuality. Some appear to develop homosexual leanings later on in life. There are not a few people who claim that each of us has the right and the ability to choose our own sexuality and to choose how to live at any given period in our lives. But it is true that there are some whose homosexual orientation is consistent from the earliest awakening of sexual desire and the general view is that they should be able to live according to what they are.

This leads to the belief that if marriage is the way that many heterosexual people will choose to live, then there should be a similar relational sphere in which homosexuals can live. So some who believe in God argue that if God has made some people homosexual then it is reasonable to believe that he intends them to live according to the way he has made them in a stable, loving relationship. This is not the place to argue this it is simply to note that this seems to many people to be a logical way to think and that there are professing Christians who take this position and indeed act upon it in their personal lives.

In this situation churches and Christians have to maintain a consistent testimony. On the one hand we have a gospel to make known to all, and it is to be done with compassion, understanding, love and faithfulness. On the other we cannot compromise biblical standards of behaviour. Whether people will accept it or not, all are going to be judged one day and we cannot remain silent when we know that this is the case and when we know the remedy that God has provided. Christians need great wisdom and understanding in trying to present the gospel to those of another faith or culture, and we need the same in our own diverse society.

There may be people who do not think of the Christian gospel as good news, but rather as bad news. Consider those who are quite outside the orbit of the churches, who have settled into the current homosexual culture that is now generally socially acceptable. What impression do they receive of evangelical Christianity from the media or from Christian literature? Do they have any idea that we believe we have a message of mercy that will do them good? Suppose they were to come in to a service and on that occasion homosexuality was referred to in the sermon. What would they hear, and what effect would it be likely to have on them?

It is probable that there are more young people—and older ones, too—struggling with their sexual identity in evangelical churches than most of us realise. In most cases it is a struggle that is conducted in secret, and the last thing they want is for anyone to know about it. Unfortunately their very sensitivity means they are likely to pick up on anything that seems to them to be negative and condemnatory. When such people do reveal their struggles and ask for help, in many cases they will be treated with considerable sympathy and understanding. And in many churches it would be just the same for those who come in from outside. When confronted with actual people we usually try to adopt a wise and compassionate approach. But there is a danger that in wanting to uphold biblical standards we might speak forcefully and simply condemn in public preaching, forgetting that sinners 'out there' are actually the congregation 'in here'.

Against this background this book has seven diverse chapters. It considers the attitude of the Christian church to homosexuality historically and then looks at the subject from a medical perspective. After this it turns to the biblical evidence, considering sexuality and marriage first of all and then focusing on the key biblical passages. The next two chapters deal firstly with recent legislation and how this impinges on churches and Christians and then how the local church should respond pastorally to homosexuals. The final chapter tells the story of one individual and introduces the work of True Freedom Trust.

Learning from the past

Kenneth Brownell

On 7 March 2004 Gene Robinson was consecrated as the bishop of the New Hampshire diocese of the Episcopal Church in the United States. What made this event so momentous was that Robinson, a divorced father of two, was and remains a practising homosexual who lives with his male partner. Most bishops in the Episcopal Church supported Robinson's consecration, but some did not. Indeed, throughout the Anglican Communion the event sparked off a controversy that shows no sign of abating. The predominantly conservative churches in Africa and Asia as well as evangelicals and traditionalists in Britain, Australia and Canada want the American church to be brought to heel on the matter. But it is not only the American church. In the Anglican Church of Canada the diocese of New Westminster has sanctioned the blessing of same-sex partnerships, and in the Church of England a homosexual, Jeffrey Johns, was appointed as Bishop of Reading, although because of opposition he withdrew from the appointment. But the issue is bigger than several appointments and changes in church practice. The issue of homosexuality is being hotly debated at every level of church life. This is not only a problem in the Anglican Communion. Although less in the news, other denominations in the western world are having to deal with this issue. Some, such as the United Church of Christ in the United States, sanction the ordination of homosexuals as well as homosexual practice in general. Others, such as the United Methodist Church in the United States and the United Reformed Church in Great Britain, have drawn back from doing so. On a much more personal level there are many people in churches of all denominations wrestling with this issue, either because they are homosexuals or know people who are.

How have we got to this point in the western church? Christians in Africa and Asia are amazed that we have. The purpose of this chapter is simply to trace the path that led to the consecration of Gene Robinson and all that it represents. For evangelical Christians who want to remain faithful to

Scripture and to the historic teaching of the church, homosexuality presents a great challenge. It is important for us to know how Christians in previous generations looked at this matter, and to learn from them as we try to obey God in very different circumstances today.

Of course, there are some people for whom the consecration of Gene Robinson was neither distressing nor surprising. For them it indicated that the church was at long last returning to the attitude it originally had concerning homosexual behaviour. Until relatively recently it was generally assumed that the church had always been opposed to sexual activity between people of the same gender and it was also assumed that this position was firmly based on the teaching of the Bible. Today there is an increasing number of people who question this assumption. The first significant dissent from the prevailing view came in 1955 with the publication of D. Sherwin Bailey's book *Homosexuality and the Western Christian Tradition*.[1] Bailey's thesis is that the traditional Christian hostility to homosexual activity is built on a misunderstanding of Genesis 19 and the sin of Sodom. Rather than being guilty of wanting to homosexually rape Lot's visitors, the men of Sodom were guilty of inhospitality.[2] Others have followed the path Bailey pioneered, the most significant to date being Professor John Boswell of Yale University. In two remarkable books, *Christianity, Social Tolerance and Homosexuality: Gay People in Western Europe from the Beginning of the Christian Era to the Fourteenth Century* (1989) and *The Marriage of Likeness: Same Sex Unions in pre-Modern Europe* (1994),[3] Professor Boswell has sought completely to revise the way in which we understand homosexuality historically. Boswell contends that since the fourteenth century the church has misunderstood the New Testament teaching and has turned away from an earlier, more tolerant view of homosexuality. While Boswell's conclusions, and indeed his handling of the historical material, have been challenged by fellow academics, his views have been widely accepted in many church circles. For many, Boswell has proved the case that the church must return to a more open and tolerant attitude to homosexuality and even recognise same-sex marriages.[4] An example is Michael Vasey's *Strangers and Friends* (1995) which is the first book in Great Britain written by a professing evangelical to advocate the recognition of same-sex relationships.[5]

In surveying the history of Christian attitudes to homosexuality I will have to take into account this revisionist thinking. Given the limits of space I will have to be somewhat selective and perhaps superficial in my treatment. Nevertheless, I will show that there is no need to revise our understanding of the church's historic position on the practice of homosexuality, but rather every reason to maintain it in spite of the strong cultural pressure to the contrary.

The early church (100–600)

Christianity was born into a social context in which male homosexuality was tolerated and widely practised. The homosexuality or bisexuality of many of the emperors is well known, but the evidence for male prostitution shows that homosexuality was not confined to the higher reaches of society. In Roman society it was permitted for men freely to engage in sexual activity with inferiors, especially with slaves.[6] There were limits, however, and homosexuality involving children (pederasty) was not tolerated legally or socially. Although there were relatively few laws relating to homosexuality before the fourth century AD, those that did exist were concerned primarily with pederasty. This was the background against which Paul wrote his letters and the early fathers taught. Subsequent chapters will deal with the biblical teaching on homosexuality, but at this point it is important to see that there is a clear continuity between the teaching of the New Testament and that of the early church. The early church fathers condemned the practice of homosexuality just as roundly as did the apostle Paul. The social historian Eva Cantarella, a leading authority in this area, writes: 'The fact that Christian teaching condemned homosexuality from the beginning is a fact (although sometimes denied) that emerges with absolute clarity from the sources.' She goes on to write that 'Paul's preaching … lays the foundation for a new sexual ethic, which Christian writers in the following centuries were to repeat with decisive certainty, without any concession or hesitation'.[7]

What is the evidence for this? There are a number of references to homosexuality in some of the earliest Christian writings. In the *Didache* or the *Teaching of the Twelve Apostles* (second to third centuries) there is a household code similar to that in the New Testament letters. Here homosexual activity involving young boys is prohibited: 'Do not murder; do not commit adultery; do not corrupt boys; do not fornicate; do not practise magic ...'[8] Later in the fourth century the *Apostolical Constitutions* of the Syrian Church incorporated and expanded the *Didache:* 'You shall not corrupt boys; for this wickedness is contrary to nature, and arose from Sodom, which was therefore entirely consumed with fire sent from God. Let such a one be accursed and all the people shall say "Amen".'[9] In his *Apology* (c.155 AD) Justin Martyr (d.165) mentions how Christians did not give away their children as pagans often did 'for the purpose of sodomy'.[10] The Latin lawyer and theologian Tertullian (c.160–c.220) writes in *Against Marcion* of how God 'punishes with death both sacrilegious incest and the portentous madness of lust against male persons and cattle'. In his later Montanist period Tertullian was even more forthright in his condemnation: '... all other frenzies of the lusts that exceed the laws of nature and are impious towards both [human] bodies and the sexes, we banish, not only from the threshold but also from all shelter of the Church, for they are not sins so much as monstrosities.'[11] Lactantius (c.240–c.320) wrote in his *Divine Institutes* that when God created two sexes he 'placed in them the desire of each other and joy in union. So he put in bodies the most ardent desire of all living things, so that they might rush most avidly into those emotions and be able by this means to propagate and increase their kind'. This was the divine order and the devil opposes it by tempting people into sexual immorality. 'The [devil] has even joined males and has contrived abominable intercourse against nature and against the institution of God.'[12]

Slowly the cultural environment around the church began to change. In the later Roman empire homosexual practice was tolerated less and less, especially among the urban middle classes. New laws proscribing homosexuality appeared from the third century onwards. Why did this change occur? Historians attribute the change in part to the dominance of Christianity by the fourth century. Eva Cantarella writes that '[by] Justinian's time, the patristic writers had worked out a theology of sexuality which condemned relationships between persons of the same sex as "against nature"'. She notes that there was also a profound change in pagan morality in this period 'from bisexuality, based on aggressive gratification into heterosexuality based on reproduction'. In short, chastity became a virtue. There are a number of reasons for this, but one is the formative influence of Christianity on the culture as it sought 'to introduce a different sexual ethic'.[13]

Among the most influential theologians in this later period were the three great Cappadocian fathers—Basil of Caesarea, his brother Gregory of Nyssa and their friend Gregory of Nazianzus—who dealt with the issue of homosexuality in their teaching. Around 375 Basil (c.330–379) wrote that 'he who is guilty of unseemliness with males will be under discipline for the same time as adulterers'.[14] One of the greatest preachers of the early church was John Chrysostom (c.345–407), given that name, 'the golden mouthed', because of his eloquence. Chrysostom was forthright in his opposition to homosexuality. When he was the principal preacher of Antioch he faced the pastoral problem of homosexual activity among the children of Christians that even their parents tolerated. In the following quotation there may be an element of rhetorical exaggeration, but it indicates something of the problems of maintaining biblical standards in a sexually permissive culture.

Those very people who have been nourished by godly doctrine, who instruct others in what they ought and ought not to do, who have heard the Scriptures brought down from heaven, these do not consort with prostitutes as fearlessly as they do with men. The fathers of the young men take this in silence: they do not try to sequester their sons, nor do they seek any remedy for this evil. None is ashamed, no one blushes, they take pride in their little game; the chaste seem to be the odd ones, and the disapproving the ones in error. If these disapprovers are insignificant, they are intimidated; if they are powerful, they are mocked and laughed at, refuted with a thousand arguments. The courts are powerless, the laws, instructions, parents, friends, teachers—all helpless.[15]

After Chrysostom became bishop of Constantinople, the imperial capital, in 398, he continued to be uncompromising in upholding biblical teaching. In his sermon on Romans 1:26–27 he calls sexual lust 'vile', but especially 'lust after males' and, referring to Sodom, sees the greatness of the sin in the fact that it 'forced hell to appear even before its time'. For Chrysostom homosexual activity was unnatural and destructive of human society. The sermon deals with the whole issue of homosexuality very thoroughly and at great length.[16]

Chrysostom's contemporary Augustine (354–430), bishop of Hippo in north Africa, was equally strong in his opposition. Augustine is one of the towering theological figures of the Christian church and one of the most formative intellectual influences on western culture. In his *Confessions* he comments on homosexuality in the context of discussing his own struggle with heterosexual lust as a young man:

Can it be wrong for any of us at any time or in any place to love God with his whole heart, and with his whole soul, and with his whole mind, and to love his neighbour as himself? Therefore, vicious deeds that are contrary to nature, are everywhere and always detested and punished, such as were those of the men of Sodom. Even if all nations should do these deeds, they would all be held in equal guilt under the divine law, for it has not made men in such fashion that they should use one another in this way. For in truth society itself, which must obtain between God and us, is violated, when the nature of which he is author is perverted by a polluted lust.[17]

In his greatest work, *The City of God,* Augustine returns to this theme. Speaking of Sodom he says:

It was a place where sexual promiscuity among males had grown into a custom so prevalent that it received the kind of sanction generally afforded by law to other activities. But the punishment of the men of Sodom was a foretaste of the divine judgment to come. And there is a special significance that those who were being rescued by the angels were forbidden to look back. Does it not tell us that we must not return in thought to the old life, which is sloughed off when a man is reborn by grace, if we look to escape the final judgment?[18]

The teaching of the early fathers was reflected in official enactments of church councils. The Council of Elvira in Spain in 305–6 forbade practising homosexuals to take communion. A few years later in 314 the Council of Ancyra (Ankara) addressed the issue of those who 'commit defilement with animals or males'. Much later the second Council of Tours in 567 sought more rigorously to enforce the Rule of St Benedict which among forbade monks to sleep in the same bed.[19] Apparently there ...m with homosexuality in the monasteries that had begun to spread throughout Christendom from the fourth century onwards. Basil of Caesarea had to counsel monks under his supervision to avoid situations in which they might be tempted in this area.[20]

It is clear from this brief survey that the early church was opposed to the practice of homosexuality for four reasons: it was harmful to young boys; it was against nature; it was the sin for which Sodom was punished by fire, and it was contrary to the divine order as revealed in Scripture. This would remain the church's basic position until the present day.

Recently some historians have challenged this interpretation of the early church's attitude towards homosexuality. In particular, John Boswell has tried to show that the early church was far more tolerant than has been commonly thought. Boswell's stated intention is to show that the church has not always been opposed to homosexual behaviour. He claims, for example, that there were some well-known practising homosexual Christians such as Paulinus of Nola and his friend Arsonius. His evidence for this is the affectionate way in which they addressed each other in their letters. He claims that early Christians practised homosexual acts, based largely on the evidence of accusations brought against Christians by their opponents. He also subjects the relevant passages from the early fathers to intense critical scrutiny in an attempt to relativise their force.[21] In his book *The Marriage of Likeness,* Boswell argues that the early church sanctioned same-sex 'marriages' for which there were appropriate liturgies.[22]

Boswell's argument is very sophisticated, but also very questionable. Fellow historians have challenged his methods and questioned his conclusions. He has been accused of 'advocacy scholarship' in trying to use history to support a contemporary cause, in this case homosexual rights. The Roman Catholic theologian and cultural commentator John Richard Neuhaus describes Boswell's method in this way:

Boswell's reading of early Christian and medieval history [like his interpretation of the biblical texts] turns up what he wants to find. Christian history is a multifarious affair, and it does not take much sniffing around to discover frequent instances of what is best described as hanky-panky. The discovery process is facilitated if one goes through history with what is aptly described as narrow-eyed prurience, interpreting every expression of intense affection between men as proof that they were 'gay' … Boswell rummages through Christian history and triumphantly comes up with the conclusion, 'They were everywhere'. Probably at all times in Christian history one can find instances of homosexual behaviour. And it is probably true that at some times more than others such behaviour was viewed with 'tolerance', in that it was treated with a wink and a nudge … Despite his assiduous efforts, what Boswell's historical scavenger hunt does not produce is any evidence whatever that authoritative Christian teaching ever departed from the recognition that homosexual acts were morally wrong.[23]

Historians in the field concur. The distinguished evangelical church historian David Wright has written extensively on this matter and concludes that, while influential, Boswell's book is 'highly misleading'.[24] In an important article, 'Early Christian Attitudes to Homosexuality', Wright says, 'Boswell's edifice is certainly impressive, but closer acquaintance … exposes ever widening cracks,' and concludes after examining his case that, 'Boswell's book provides in the end of the day not one firm piece of evidence that the teaching mind of the early church countenanced homosexual activity'. Contrary to what some think the early fathers were not obsessed with the subject or with singling out active homosexuals, 'but what they do say leaves little room for debate: homosexual behaviour was contrary to the will of God as expressed in Scripture and nature'.[25] The American Episcopalian historian J.R. Wright questions, among other things, Boswell's treatment of the patristic material. In particular he points out that Boswell neglected to consult 'a large body of critical writing that would not lend support to his cause', by which he means the *Biblia Patristica*, a large computerised index of the commentaries of the early fathers on the New Testament. He concludes that Boswell's case is 'undemonstrated' and therefore a shaky foundation from which to change the historic teaching and practice of the church.[26]

The medieval period (600–1500)

The doctrinal consensus of the early church concerning homosexuality was maintained throughout the medieval period. During this period Christianity dominated everything in most of Europe, and Christian standards became the norm of acceptable moral behaviour. There was relatively little legislation relating to homosexuality. Sherwin Bailey says that over a period of 1,000 years there were only 100 or so items of legislation in the whole of Europe which would seem to indicate that by and large the authorities in church and state were not overly concerned with homosexuality. Bailey writes:

[The homosexual] is certainly denounced as one guilty of very grave sin, but he is not singled out for sadistic persecution; he is offered reconciliation with God and man through the Church's penitential discipline, but if he refuses the means of grace, he has to take the eternal consequences and the temporal consequences of his crime.[27]

The synods of the church were somewhat more concerned about homosexuality. The sixteenth Council of Toledo in 693 condemned homosexual practice. In his opening address to the assembled clergy, the Visogothic ruler Egica said, 'Among other matters, see that you determine to extirpate that obscene crime committed by those who lie with males.' And so the council tried to do. In its third decree it said: '... if any one of those males who commit this vile practice against nature with other males is a bishop, a priest or a deacon, he shall be degraded from the dignity of his order, and shall remain in perpetual exile, struck down by damnation.' In a supplementary edict the council said, 'Certainly we strive to abolish the detestable outrage of that lust by the filthy uncleanness of which men do not fear to defile other men in the unlawful act of sodomy.' Other enactments against homosexuality include the Ordinance of Aix-en-Chapelle of 789, the decrees of the Council of London of 1102 and a canon of the Third Lateran Council of 1179 which became a benchmark for subsequent ecclesiastical legislation. The most severe ecclesiastical legislation is to be found in the canons of the Council of Naplouse of 1120 that demanded execution by burning for practising homosexuals.[28]

Far more significant for understanding the attitude of the church towards homosexuality in the medieval period are the penitentials. Originating in the Celtic church of Ireland and Wales and eventually spreading to the continent, penitentials were handbooks for confessors that provided schedules of penances for various sins. Almost every conceivable sin known to man is covered, including homosexuality. Some have seen the detailed treatment of homosexual offences as evidence that homosexuality was widespread, particularly within monastic communities. This is a mistake. The penitentials simply try to cover all contingencies that a priest might face in the confessional. Homosexuality is invariably seen as a sin, but not one qualitatively worse than many others. Penances were applied according to the type of homosexual sin that ranged from kissing to sodomy. The penances were also more severe for clergy than for laymen (the higher the office the more severe the penalty), and for men than for women. The concern of the penitentials is always pastoral and aims at restoration rather than punishment. A good example is the penitential regulation of Pope Gregory III (731–741) that, as Bailey points out, 'well expresses ... the general Christian attitude at the time towards such acts'.

If any ordained person has been defiled with the crime of sodomy, which is described as a vice so abominable in the sight of God that the cities in which its practitioners dwelt were appointed for destruction by fire and brimstone, let him do penance for ten years, according to the ancient rule. Some, however, being more humanely disposed, have fixed the term at seven years. Those also who are ignorant of the gravity of the offence are assigned three years in which to do penance. As for boys who know that they are indulging in this practice, it behoves them to hasten to amend; let them do penance for fifty days, and in addition let them be beaten with rods; for it is necessary that the crop which has brought forth bad fruit be cut down.[29]

The area where considerable attention has been focused in the contemporary debate on homosexuality is in the medieval phenomenon known as 'spiritual' or 'passionate' friendships. Boswell puts great weight on this in making his case that the church had a more tolerant attitude towards homosexuality before the fourteenth century. He cites, for example, the circle of friends around Alcuin (735?–804) in the court of Charlemagne in the eighth century. Apparently they used affectionate pet names among themselves and wrote love poems for one another. Alcuin himself, one of the most learned and devout men of his age, could write to a bishop in these terms, 'I think of your love and friendship with such sweet memories … that I long for that lovely time when I may be able to clutch the neck of your sweetness with the fingers of my desires.'[30] Anselm (1093–1109), one of the church's greatest theologians and the author of the classic on the atonement *Cur deus homo?* (*Why did God become man?*), would customarily address his correspondents, 'Beloved Lover', and could write to one correspondent, 'Wherever you go my love follows you, and wherever I remain my desire embraces you … How can I forget you? He who is imprinted on my heart like a seal on wax—how could he be removed from my memory?'[31] But the most significant writer in this strain was Aelred of Rievaulx who wrote the classic work *On Spiritual Friendship*. Aelred was a highly respected abbot whose monastery at Rievaulx in England was known for its high standard of monastic discipline. He wrote his book in response to a question about nurturing friendships among monks, but it is well worth reading by anyone wanting to reflect on the character of genuine friendship within a Christian framework. Among other things Aelred warned his readers of the danger of carnality in friendship, although it is difficult to know if he is referring here to sexual attraction or more broadly to other passions. He speaks of how passing 'into the other, as it were, coming into close contact with the sweetness of Christ himself, the friend begins to taste his sweetness and to experience his charm. Thus ascending from the holy love with which he embraces a friend to that with which he embraces Christ, he will joyfully partake in abundance of the spiritual fruit of friendship awaiting the fullness of all things in the life to come.'[32] Aelred mentions his own experience of friendship as a young monk in such a way that some, such as Boswell, have claimed that he was a homosexual, albeit a celibate one. He wrote that their friendship grew

until we attained that stage at which we had one mind and one soul, to will and not to will alike … For I deemed my heart in a fashion his, and his mine, and he felt in like manner towards me … He was the refuge of my spirit, the sweet solace of my griefs, whose heart of love received me when fatigued with labours, whose counsel refreshed me when plunged in sadness and grief … What more is there, then, that I can say? Was it not a foretaste of blessedness thus to love and thus to be loved?[33]

Clearly for Aelred friendships between men could be deeply emotional and could involve passionate affections. 'Feelings are not ours to command,' he wrote. 'We are attracted to some against our will, while towards others we can never experience a spontaneous affection.'

What then are we to make of these passionate friendships? Are they evidence of a more tolerant attitude towards homosexuality in the early Middle Ages? It is not difficult to see why Boswell and others have tried to build their case on these friendships. Certainly to our ears the almost erotic language used is very strange indeed. But such language was a common form of address in this period. Speaking of the alleged homosexual relationship of Edward II and Piers Galveston, Caroline Bingham writes that Edward II:

lived in a period when an intimate friendship between two men was a formal relationship governed by a code of rules like that of courtly love. Such a relationship was the subject of the Anglo-Norman romance, *Amis and Amilou*. Two friends could be described as '*leals amants*' (loyal lovers) and their relationship as '*fyne amor*', but homosexuality was completely outside the convention.[34]

It is not coincidental that Bernard of Clairvaux wrote his long allegorical commentary on the Song of Songs in the same period in which he expounds the Christian's relationship to Christ through the metaphor of the courtship and marriage of the lover and his beloved. Is it surprising that a similar idiom was used by Aelred and others to speak of male friendships without any suggestion of sexual passion? Christopher Brooke speaks of the 'shifting attitudes to human love' in twelfth-century Europe and writes: 'One tradition stemming from the ancient world saw human affection issuing in real comradeship, as chiefly to be found in the relationship of man to man.' He goes on to mention Bernard and how he could 'use a language of affection which might be supposed homosexual—but one has only to contemplate the use he makes of erotic imagery in his *Sermon on the Song of Songs* to realise that metaphor was to him a wholly abstract thing—as to many writers of the 11th and 12th centuries, a fact which renders their full meaning peculiarly difficult to grasp.'[35]

Confirmation of this is seen in the numerous references in this period to the friendships of David and Jonathan, and Jesus and the 'beloved disciple', which were highly emotional and even physical without the remotest suggestion of homosexuality. Perhaps the difficulty is not so much with the language of friendship in the twelfth century, but the shallowness of friendship in the twenty-first century. Today many cannot think of intimate same-sex relationships without thinking about sex.

No doubt there were instances of homosexual behaviour among the clergy in the medieval period. Boswell cites several cases that may well have been true, but these tell us nothing more about the church's official attitude towards homosexuality than do moral lapses or even aberrant teaching by church leaders today.[36] There were certainly periods when Christian leaders felt that homosexuality was a widespread problem. Earlier in the period Boniface (c.680–754), the great missionary to the Germans, complained in a letter to the King of Mercia that '… the people of England have been living a shameful life, despising lawful marriages, committing adultery, and lusting after the people of Sodom'.[37] Though disputed by Boswell, the last reference was probably to homosexuality. In the twelfth century Anselm wrote to a colleague after the Council of London had decreed against homosexuality that 'this sin has hitherto been so public that hardly anyone is embarrassed by it, and many have therefore fallen into it because they are unaware of its seriousness'.[38] The French social historian Henri Bresc points out that the thirteenth century was obsessed with sexual vice in general and homosexuality in particular and that during the century there seems to have been an increase in prosecutions of homosexuals.[39] As with many things there may have been periods when homosexuality was fashionable, especially among the elite classes to which the higher clergy belonged. With the revival of classical learning in the Renaissance there seems to have also been a revival of what the Romans called 'Greek love'. Homosexuality in the academies of Rome and other Italian universities was alleged to be rife in the late fifteenth century. John D'Amico writes that for 'some [priests] the imposed celibacy of the clerical state may have exacerbated individual tendencies' and that the name Socrates 'was a byword for more than wisdom in the Renaissance'.[40] Visitors to Italy noted the number of male prostitutes. Not surprisingly Bernardino of Siena and Savonarola (1452–1498) preached against this vice in their campaigns for ecclesiastical and social reform. Between 1348 and

1461 there were some fifty court cases related to homosexuality in Florence, but there is little evidence that homosexuals in any large numbers were ever put to death there or elsewhere and most historians do not think that homosexuality was very widespread.[41]

But, whatever lapses there were, the church maintained her teaching on homosexuality. In addition to the penitentials and canon law the church's theologians consistently taught that homosexual activity was sinful. The most extreme example of this was a book entitled *Liber Gomorrhianus* by Peter Damiani (1007–1072). Peter considered the penitentials far too lenient in relation to homosexuality and in violent language recommended that offenders be punished without mitigation.[42] The book was not well received; the authorities, while not favourably disposed towards homosexuality, preferred to deal with the problem more dispassionately and pastorally. Such was the approach of Albertus Magnus (c.1193–1280) and his even greater protégé Thomas Aquinas (1225–1274), the foremost of all medieval theologians. In several places in his *Summa Theologiae* Thomas deals with homosexuality. His principal objection was that homosexuality is against Scripture, reason and nature.

Thomas's understanding of nature and natural law was a synthesis of biblical teaching and Aristotelian philosophy. As Arthur Holmes explains, 'Natural law is inherent in the essence of created things, in the good ends that are natural for all humans to pursue, the potential that humans generically share.'[43] So Thomas opposed homosexuality both by citing texts such as Leviticus 19:16 and by showing that there are some sins contrary to nature such 'as ... those that run counter to the intercourse of males and females natural to animals, and so are peculiarly qualified as unnatural vices'. He wrote that a 'lustful man intends sex for pleasure, not human fruitfulness, and he can experience this without a generative act; this is what he seeks in unnatural vice'; in other words homosexuality was by definition unfruitful and therefore unnatural. Against the argument that freely consented homosexual coitus was not as serious as other sins since it harmed no one other than the participants, Thomas argued that it was an injury done to God since it contravened his natural order.[44] The thinking of Thomas was reflected in the literature of the period. Alain de Lille's book *De Plancto Naturae* (*The Complaint of Nature*) excoriated the homosexuality he felt was so prevalent in the late thirteenth century. His theme was 'the complaint of Nature against all who deviate from the natural modes of conduct and intercourse, by the observance of which Man glorifies his Creator and attains true happiness and fulfilment in life'.[45] All this Boswell interprets as great intellectual change that turned the church away from its previously more open attitude to homosexuality to a more hostile and repressive one.[46] I suggest that although the position was more refined and sophisticated it was nevertheless fundamentally the same as the church had always held.

The Reformation period to the Victorian era (1500–1900)

We have had to spend considerable time looking at the attitude towards homosexuality of the early and medieval church since this is the point where Boswell and others have challenged the traditional position of the church. From now on we can move much faster. In the early sixteenth century the western church experienced the upheaval of the Reformation as many people rediscovered the gospel. But whatever the differences between Roman Catholics and Protestants over doctrine, all were agreed that homosexuality was sinful and socially destructive. For our purposes I will concentrate on the thinking of Protestant theologians, but the position of the Roman Church should not be forgotten.

Homosexuality was not a major concern of the reformers. Contrary to modern images of ranting preachers seeking to intrude into every corner of people's private lives, the Protestant leaders of the sixteenth and seventeenth centuries were rather sparing in their references to homosexuality and, when they had to deal with it, did so with some distaste. When lecturing on Genesis at Wittenburg, Martin Luther (1483–1546) came to chapter 19 and the account of Sodom and Gomorrah with a very heavy heart. It gave him no pleasure to speak of God's wrath or of such an unseemly sin. He says that

Moses proceeds with a description of a terrible sin. I for my part do not enjoy dealing with this passage, because so far the ears of Germans are innocent and uncontaminated by this monstrous depravity; for even though this disgrace, like other sins, has crept in through an ungodly soldier and a lewd merchant, still the rest of the people are unaware of what is being done in secret ... [Nevertheless] this passage contains a necessary and profitable doctrine. We see that when sins become the fashion and human beings smugly indulge in them, the punishment of God follows immediately ... The heinous conduct of the people of Sodom is extraordinary inasmuch as they departed from the natural passion and longing of the male for the female, which was implanted into nature by God, and desired what is altogether contrary to nature. Whence comes the perversity? Undoubtedly from Satan, who, after people have turned away from the fear of God, so powerfully suppresses nature that he blots out the natural desire and stirs up a desire that is contrary to nature.

Luther was shocked by the openness and shamelessness of this sin and mentions his own experience of visiting Rome where he saw 'cardinals who were esteemed highly as saints because they were content to associate with women'. Luther was always fearful of social anarchy and sought to apply to his hearers the lesson of Sodom's destruction:

Therefore if the Lord had not brought on the punishment which they deserved, the government would gradually have collapsed and could not have continued to exist. For if you do away with the marriage bond and permit promiscuous passions, the laws and all decency go to ruin together with discipline. But when these are destroyed, no government remains; only beastliness and savagery are left. Therefore as an example for others the Lord was compelled to inflict punishment and to check the madness that was raging beyond measure.[47]

In commenting on Romans 1:24, Luther related the sin of homosexuality to the spiritual and moral decay of society: 'From this text we may therefore deduce that if someone surrenders to these passions, it is a sure sign that he has left the worship of God and has worshipped an idol, or he has turned the truth of God into a lie.'[48] Luther's views need to be seen against the background of a desire on the one hand to redress lax discipline of sexual sins in the Catholic Church and on the other to re-establish the divine calling of marriage and family life. The Lutheran theologian Andreas Musculus wrote of how the devil hates marriage and uses homosexuality to destroy it.[49]

The Genevan reformer John Calvin (1509–1564) adopted the same attitude as Luther. In his commentary on Genesis 19 he calls homosexuality 'an abominable sin' and exclaims:

How blind and impetuous is their lust; since without shame they rush together like brute animals! How great their ferocity and cruelty; since they reproachfully threaten the holy man and proceed to all extremities ... But when the sense of shame is overcome, and the reins are given to lust, a vile and outrageous barbarism succeeds and many kinds of sins are blended together so that a most confused chaos is the result.[50]

Interestingly Calvin does not interpret the word 'know' in verse 5 to mean sexual knowledge, but rather social acquaintance as many of the revisionists would prefer to understand it. Nevertheless, it is clear that Calvin believes that homosexuality was the primary sin for which Sodom was punished. In his commentary on Romans 1:26 Calvin speaks of '... the dreadful crime of unnatural lust' and how 'it appears that they not only abandoned themselves to beastly lusts, became degraded beyond the beasts, since they reversed the natural order'.[51] In his commentary on 1 Corinthians 6:9 he writes of homosexuality as 'the most abominable of all the monstrous pollution which was but too prevalent in Greece'.[52] Calvin's colleague Heinrich Bullinger (1504–1575), the successor to Zwingli in Zurich, was equally forthright. Bullinger is significant because of the great influence of his doctrinal sermons, *The Decades,* in England where they were recommended reading for the clergy of the newly reformed Church of England. Bullinger writes:

The abominable sin of sodomy, and meddling with beasts, also is plainly forbidden, against which we have most evident and express laws set down in the 18th and 19th chapters of Leviticus. We have also a very severe, but yet a most just, punishment laid by God himself upon the pates of the detestable Sodomites; for with fire and stinking brimstone sent down from heaven, he consumed those filthy men to dust and ashes.[53]

It is clear then from these examples that the reformers maintained the ancient teaching of the church on homosexuality. It is surprising, therefore, to discover that the great Protestant confessions of the sixteenth and seventeenth centuries do not, with one exception, mention homosexuality.

Why is this? In part it is because, for the reformers and their successors, the issue was so clear that it did not need to be mentioned, but it is also because they were not particularly obsessed with the issue. The one exception is the *Heidelberg Catechism* that in Question and Answer 87 says:

Question: Can those who do not turn to God from their ungrateful, impenitent life be saved?

Answer: Most certainly not! Scripture says, Surely you know that the unjust never come into possession of the kingdom of God. Make no mistake: no fornicator or idolater, none who are guilty either of adultery or homosexual perversion, no thieves or grabbers or drunkards or slanderers or swindlers, will possess the kingdom of God.

The teaching and emphasis of the reformers was maintained in succeeding generations. The Puritan Thomas Goodwin called homosexuality or sodomy an 'unnatural uncleanness'.[54] Later David Clarkson sought to illustrate the baleful effects of Roman Catholic teaching in his *Practical Divinity of the Papists discovered to be destructive of Christianity and Men's Souls* by mentioning how prevalent sodomy was in Italy where unmarried priests were so thick on the ground.[55] In his great compendium of Christian ethics, *The Christian Directory*, Richard Baxter spoke of the 'filthy lusts' of the Sodomites and put homosexual sin in the same category as fornication.[56] The great Puritan commentator Matthew Henry leaves us in no doubt in his comment on Genesis 19:4:

It was the most unnatural and abominable wickedness that they were now set upon, a sin that still bears their name, and is called Sodomy. They were carried headlong by those vile affections (Romans 1:26–27) which are worse than brutish, and the eternal reproach of the human nature, and which cannot be thought of without horror by those who have the least spark of virtue, and any remains of natural light and conscience. Note, those that allow themselves in unnatural uncleanness, are marked for the vengeance of eternal fire.

He wrote that by force 'they proclaim their war with virtue and bid open defiance to it'.[57] He makes a similar comment on Judges 19:22–30 when he says that the men of the town sought 'the gratification of that unnatural and brutish lust, that was expressly forbidden in the Law of Moses and called an abomination'.[58] In his very influential work *Holy Living and Holy Dying* Bishop Jeremy Taylor considered all 'who are adulterous, incestuous, sodomitical, or commit fornication' as violators of the seventh commandment.[59] Later in the eighteenth century the Baptist pastor and theologian Andrew Fuller wrote that men of Sodom sought not only to rob and insult Lot's guests 'but to perpetrate a species of crime too shocking and detestable to be named'.[60]

The teaching of the reformers and Puritans on homosexuality needs to be seen in its social context. From the sixteenth to the eighteenth centuries homosexuality was at times believed to be rampant and considered destructive to the social order, not least because it might provoke God's judgement. Periodically it came to be considered fashionable in aristocratic circles and was known to exist in the courts of Elizabeth I and James I/VI and later of Charles II. The period after the Restoration in 1660 was morally very relaxed and therefore a play such as John Wilmot's *The Quintessence of Debauchery,* which had sodomy as its theme, would not have been too shocking in polite London society. The Duchess of Orleans could comment in 1698 that 'nothing is more ordinary in England than this unnatural vice' and Thomas Bray could lament in *For God or Satan* that 'the sodomites are invading the land'. In the late eighteenth century homosexuality was again fashionable among the upper classes. That acute social observer Mrs Thrale commented in 1781 that it was 'now so modish' and in 1790 that 'there is a strange propensity in England for these unspeakable crimes'. The papers of the day carried detailed reports of sodomy trials. Not surprisingly laws were introduced in England and elsewhere proscribing homosexuality. Henry VIII removed jurisdiction for homosexual offences from the church to the state and thereby made it a criminal act. In New England, where Puritanism shaped society in a biblical mould, homosexuality became a capital offence.[61] But this was not unique to New England or even to Protestant nations. During this period there were a number of campaigns against homosexuality in both Protestant and Catholic countries. For example, in the 1730s there was a particularly well-documented campaign in the Netherlands where people were shocked by revelations of the extent of the homosexual underworld and felt that the republic was in danger of being overwhelmed by immorality of the grossest kind. Sodom was the theme of much Dutch Calvinist preaching during this period.[62] There were similar campaigns in Venice, Spain and France. Yet in all this it must be said that in Britain and America homosexuality does not seem to have been widespread enough to have made it an issue of great concern for Christian leaders. They maintained the orthodox tradition when the issue arose, but otherwise tended not to discuss it.

During the nineteenth century in Britain and America there was a renewed emphasis in society on marriage and family life, largely because of the profound influence of evangelical Christianity in the wake of the revivals of the eighteenth and early nineteenth centuries. Homosexuality was considered deviant and homosexuals were socially ostracised. The trial of Oscar Wilde in 1895 was a great scandal in late Victorian England, but it was also an exposure of a measure of hypocrisy and a revelation of a homosexual subculture. Homosexuality was not unknown in English public schools and in cities like London homosexual prostitutes were common, many of whom were boys or young men. Some Christians were concerned about this and in 1883 established the White Cross Society which became the White Cross League in 1891. The New Testament scholar Bishop Lightfoot and Bishop Randall Davidson (who later became Archbishop of Canterbury) and his wife were very involved in this work.[63]

The twentieth century

The consensus of Christian teaching in the early twentieth century remained opposed to homosexual activity. Sometimes this could be little more than prudish as seen in the comment of the *Interpreter's Bible* in 1954 on Romans 1:27: 'The subject is one which in honesty must be faced, but on which no man of fine feeling would care to linger.'[64] Linger the commentator doesn't; he moves quickly on to more edifying matters. More robust was Karl Barth's treatment of homosexuality in his monumental *Church Dogmatics*. Speaking of homosexuality he says:

This is the physical, psychological and social sickness, the phenomenon of perversion, decadence and decay, which can emerge when men refuse to admit the validity of the divine command … In Romans 1 Paul connected it with idolatry, with changing the truth of God into a lie, with the adoration of the creature instead of the Creator (v.25) … From the refusal to recognise God there follows the failure to appreciate man, and thus humanity without the fellow man. And since humanity as fellow-humanity is to be understood in its root as the togetherness of man and woman, at the root of this inhumanity there follows the ideal of a masculinity free from woman and a femininity free from man. And because nature and the Creator of nature will not be trifled with, because the despised fellow-man is still there, because the natural orientation on him is still in force, there follows the corrupt emotional and finally physical desire in which— in a sexual union which is not and cannot be genuine—man thinks that he must seek and can find in man, and woman in woman, a substitute for the despised partner … The command of God shows him irrefutably—in clear contradiction of his own theories—that as a man he can only be genuinely human with woman, or as a woman with man. In proportion as he accepts this insight, homosexuality can have no place in his life, whether in its more refined or cruder forms.[65]

As Richard Lovelace points out, 'Barth is not here affirming that true humanity is impossible outside the married state … but is simply saying that all human beings realise their humanity as they open themselves in humility to the complementary excellencies of the opposing sex …'[66] The German Lutheran theologian Helmut Thielicke thinks Barth's view somewhat superficial and insensitive. While believing homosexual activity to be contrary to God's will and therefore sinful, Thielicke nevertheless thinks that homosexuality can be a genuinely human encounter between two people and that the church must be more pastorally sensitive than it has been in dealing with it. Thielicke's understanding of the biblical material incorporates much of the revisionist interpretation favoured by those who do not see homosexual activity as sinful, but Thielicke himself does not come to that conclusion. He considers homosexuality in the light of creation and the Fall and concludes that it is a perversion in the same way that disease, suffering and pain are. No moral stigma is attached to being a homosexual as such and the church's responsibility is to help the homosexual to struggle with his or her condition and to live a celibate life if necessary.[67]

While Barth and Thielicke were writing, others were beginning to challenge the traditional Christian approach to homosexuality. This needs to be seen against a backdrop of profound cultural changes after the Second World War and changing attitudes towards homosexuality. In 1948 Alfred Kinsey published his *Sexual Behaviour in the Human Male* in which he estimated that 4% of American men were confirmed homosexuals and that 37% had had homosexual experience. These findings have been subsequently questioned but they were at the time very influential. In Britain the recommendation of the Wolfenden Report of 1957, recommending the decriminalisation of homosexuality, was enacted in 1967 as part of Roy Jenkins' programme of liberal reforms. The Gay Liberation movement effectively began in 1969 in the aftermath of the Christopher Street riots in New York with its motto 'Gay is Good' and has been gaining in strength ever since. It was only a matter of time before the American Psychiatric Association removed homosexuality from its category of mental illness in 1973. Meanwhile pressure had been mounting to lower the age of consent from eighteen and to allow open homosexuals to serve in the armed forces. In the United States—and to a lesser extent Britain—the issues surrounding homosexual rights have become a key battleground in the culture wars between social conservatives and progressives. Alan Shead of Moore College in Sydney helpfully sums up these social changes in this way:

Following the questioning of traditional values represented by the Kinsey report, the 1950s were a time of legal debate and of the beginning of a supportive homosexual community. The 1960s saw legal debate progress to legislation, and homosexual support progress to gay liberation. The movement was out of the closet. In the 1970s the gay movement worked to change society's social and moral perceptions of homosexuality. Its major breakthrough was the 1973 victory of the American Psychiatric Association: homosexuality was now officially a normal and thus morally neutral condition.[68]

It was in this social context that the church in the west began to wrestle with the question of homosexuality. This was at a time when liberal theology was ascendant in the mainline Protestant denominations after the Second

World War and when the Roman Catholic Church would experience theological upheaval after Vatican II. For many Protestants what Scripture taught was no longer the primary theological criterion in discerning the mind of God on ethical issues. An example of this is the influential book, published in 1967 by the process theologian Norman Pittenger, entitled *Time for Consent—a Christian's Approach to Homosexuality,* in which he reinterprets the key texts and refers to medical and psychological studies to make his case for a more open attitude towards homosexual behaviour. For Pittenger a homosexual relationship is justified so long as it is faithful and loving; an ethical standpoint developed more fully in the situation ethics of Joseph Fletcher.[69] In 1970 the Jesuit theologian J.J. McNeill became the first Roman Catholic advocate of acceptance of homosexual activity as morally acceptable.[70] As already noted, John Boswell published *Christianity, Social Tolerance and Homosexuality* in 1980 in which he radically reinterpreted the key biblical passages and church history prior to the fourteenth century.

By and large evangelicals have stood against the tide, but recently some have broken ranks. In the United States Letha Scanzoni and Virginia Ramey Mollenkott, two of the early evangelical feminists, argued the case for acceptance of loving homosexual relationships within the church in their 1978 book *Is the Homosexual My Neighbour?* Mollenkott has herself published in 1992 a book entitled *Sensuous Spirituality* in which she speaks of her own lesbianism and acceptance of what can only be described as a New Age version of Christianity.[71] In Britain Michael Vasey, a tutor at the historically evangelical St John's College in Durham, advocated the acceptance of faithful same-sex relationships within the church in his controversial book *Strangers and Friends.* Perhaps the most sophisticated treatment of the issue from this standpoint is the book by the Dutch Protestant philosopher Pim Pronk entitled *Against Nature—Types of Moral Argumentation Regarding Homosexuality* (1993). Pronk questions the notion maintained consistently by Christian theologians through the centuries that homosexuality is against nature and subjects this claim to very detailed philosophical examination. He admits that the biblical authors view homosexuality as a sin and nowhere see it positively, but that for him is not the point because the 'issue is not decided for any Christian by exegesis alone. The understanding of the texts is always mediated by interpretative frameworks'. Everyone, says Pronk, comes to Scripture with prior moral commitments and he concludes, 'The Bible is not … a necessary condition for knowing what good and evil is.' Ethical decisions must be decided on the basis of general revelation and not special revelation.[72]

Through much of the 1970s and 80s most of the larger mainstream denominations were in turmoil over homosexuality. The primary issue was whether or not to ordain practising homosexuals. In 1972 the first openly practising homosexual was ordained in the United Church of Christ in America. Three years later a practising lesbian was ordained by the Episcopal bishop of New York in contravention of canon law. The activities and writings of Bishop Jack Spong of Newark, New Jersey, were especially notorious in encouraging homosexuals to enter the ordained ministry. In 1979 the General Convention allowed homosexuals to be ordained so long as they were 'able and willing to conform to that which the church affirms as wholesome'. In spite of, or perhaps because of this somewhat ambiguous statement, a number of bishops and clergy continued to ordain and bless the relationships of openly practising homosexuals. Similar controversies wracked other denominations such as the United Methodist Church, the Lutheran Church of America, the United Church of Christ and the United Presbyterian Church. In 1991 the General Assembly of the latter body rejected a report that recommended full acceptance of ordained homosexuals so long as relationships were characterised by 'mutuality, honesty, consent and fidelity'. Even so the General Assembly refused to declare homosexual activity sinful or heterosexual marriage as 'the only God-ordained relationship for the expression of sexual intercourse'. That same year the journal *Christianity Today* noted that homosexuality was one of the top religious news stories.[73] That was certainly true in Britain in the following years. Yet with all this debating the main denominations have not yet positively sanctioned same-sex relationships. There is much fudge, ambiguity and inconsistency, but the historic position is still officially the position of all the main churches in the English-speaking world. In part this is due to the moral conservatism of the laity, but how long that will last in the present moral climate is impossible to say. Where there has been a significant shift has been in the Netherlands where Gereformeerde Kerken (the GKN or Reformed Churches in the Netherlands), the traditionally conservative denomination of Abraham Kuyper and Herman Bavinck, has officially approved of same-sex relationships and agreed to allow people in such relationships to enter the ministry. This issue is causing considerable distress within GKN's sister body in the United States, the Christian Reformed Church (the denomination of Louis Berkhof and William Hendriksen), where the issue of homosexuality is being hotly debated.

All of which brings us back to the consecration of Gene Robinson and the controversy surrounding it. In the latter part of the twentieth century the theological foundations of the western church have been severely undermined. This has happened in a cultural context in which homosexuality has become increasingly accepted as a legitimate lifestyle without any moral stigma. Is it all that surprising then that a practising homosexual has been consecrated as a bishop in an historically Protestant denomination? Sadly not. Is it all that surprising that same-sex marriage is being discussed and advocated in some denominations? Sadly not. Is it all that surprising that some self-confessed evangelicals now advocate homosexuality within faithful relationships? Sadly not. Those who want to remain true to Scripture and its moral standards will have to stand fast and do so confident that they are standing where countless others have stood down the centuries.

Notes

1 **D. Sherwin Bailey,** *Homosexuality and the Western Christian Tradition* (Longman, Green & Co., 1955).

2 Ibid. pp.1–28.

3 **John Boswell,** *Christianity, Social Tolerance and Homosexuality—Gay People in Western Europe from the Beginning of the Christian Era to the Fourteenth Century* (University of Chicago Press, 1989) (hereafter CSTH); and *The Marriage of Likeness—Same Sex Unions in pre-Modern Europe* (HarperCollins, 1994) (hereafter ML).

4 **John Richard Neuhaus,** 'In the case of John Boswell', *Evangelical Review of Theology,* XIX, 19, 1995, p. 65. This article was originally published in the American journal *First Things.*

5 **Michael Vasey,** *Strangers and Friends: a new exploration of homosexuality* (Hodder & Stoughton, 1995).

6 **Eva Cantarella,** *Bisexuality in the Ancient World, trans.* Carmac O. Cuilleanain, (Yale University Press, 1992), pp. 160, 162, 173; see also **Peter Coleman,** *Christian Attitudes to Homosexuality* (SPCK, 1980), p.162; **Aline Purelle,** 'Family under the Roman Empire' in *A History of the Family,* Andre Burguiere, ed. (Polity Press, 1996), p. 297; **Peter Brown,** *The Body and Society—Men, Women and Sexual Renunciation in Early Christianity* (Faber & Faber, 1988), p. 79.

7   **Cantarella,** op. cit., pp.191, 193.

8   *The Didache,* 2.2, in *Ancient Christian Writers,* VI, James A. Klest SJ, trans. (Mercier Press, 1948), pp. 16, 34.

9   *Apostolical Constitutions,* VII.3, in *Ante-Nicene Christian Library* (hereafter ANCL), XVII (T. & T. Clark, n.d.), pp. 179, 228.

10 Justin Martyr, *First Apology,* XXVII, in *ANCL* II (T. & T. Clark, 1879), p. 30.

11 Tertullian, *Against Marcion,* quoted in Bailey, p. 82.

12 Lactantius, *The Divine Institutes,* VI. 23, in *ANCL* XXI (T. & T. Clark, 1871), p. 411.

13 Cantarella, op. cit., p. 188.

14 Cantarella, op. cit., p. 14; **Sherwin Bailey**, op. cit., p. 89; **Boswell,** *CSTH,* p. 121; **Coleman,** op. cit., p. 87.

15 John Chrysostom, quoted in **Boswell,** op. cit., p. 121.

16 John Chrysostom, *Homilies on Romans,* IV (1.26–27) in John Henry Parker, *Library of the Fathers of the Holy Catholic Church,* VII, 1844, pp. 44–52.

17 Augustine, *Confessions,* III.8.15, *trans.* John K. Ryan (Doubleday & Company, 1960), p. 87.

18 Augustine, *Concerning the City of God against the Pagans,* XVI.30, *trans.* Henry Bettenson (Penguin Books, 1984), p. 692.

19 Sherwin Bailey, op. cit., pp. 86, 91; **Cantarella,** op. cit., p. 127.

20 Boswell, *CSTH,* p. 159.

21 Ibid. pp. 22, 160.

22 Boswell, *ML,* pp. 10–11, 190–191, 199.

23 Neuhaus, op. cit., pp. 66–67.

24 David F. Wright, 'Homosexuality', in *The Encyclopaedia of Early Christianity* (Garland Publishing Company, 1990), p. 435.

25 David F. Wright, 'Early Christian Attitudes to Homosexuality', *Studia Patristica,* XVIII.2, (Cistercian Publications, 1989), pp. 330, 333. Wright has also written, 'Homosexuals or Prostitutes: the meaning of arsenokoites (1 Corinthians 6:19; 1 Timothy 1:10)', *Vigiliae Christianae,* 38, 1984, pp. 125–153.

26 J.R. Wright, 'Boswell on Homosexuality; A Case Undemonstrated', *Anglican Theological Review,* LXVI.1, June 1984, pp. 87f.

27 Sherwin Bailey, op. cit., p. 99.

28 Reay Tannahill, *Sex in History* (Hamish Hamilton, 1980), p. 156; also **Sherwin Bailey**, op. cit., pp. 92–97.

29 Sherwin Bailey, op. cit., p. 106.

30 Boswell, *CSTH,* p. 190.

31 Ibid. p. 218.

32 Aelred of Rievaulx, *On Spiritual Friendship,* Mary Eugenia Laker SSND, trans. (Cistercian Publications, 1977), p. 131.

33 Ibid. p.26; also **Boswell,** *CSTH,* p. 222.

34 Caroline Bingham, *The Life and Times of Edward II* (Wiedenfeld & Nicolson, 1973), p. 54; see also **Pierre Chaplais,** *Piers Galveston—Edward II's Adoptive Brother* (Clarendon Press, 1994), pp. 11, 13.

35 Christopher N.C. Brooke, *The Medieval Idea of Marriage* (Cambridge University Press, 1989), pp. 266–7.

36 Boswell, *CSTH,* pp. 191, 238ff.

37 Coleman, p. 131.

38 Boswell, *CSTH,* p. 215.

39 Henri Bresc, 'Europe: Town and Country', in **Burguiere,** p. 452.

40 John D'Amico, *Renaissance Humanism in Papal Rome* (Johns Hopkins University Press, 1983), pp. 92–93.

41 David Greenberg, *The Construction of Homosexuality* (University of Chicago Press, 1988), pp. 305, 307; see also **Sherwin Bailey,** op. cit., p. 134.

42 Sherwin Bailey, op. cit., p. 112.

43 Arthur Holmes, 'Natural Law' in *The New Dictionary of Christian Ethics and Pastoral Theology,* **David J. Atkinson** and **David H. Field** (eds) (Inter-Varsity Press, 1995), p. 619.

44 Thomas Aquinas, *Summa Theologiae,* 20:25; 28:84; 43:47; 43:245 (Blackfriars in association with Eyre & Spottiswoode, 1964–1980); see also **Sherwin Bailey,** op. cit., p. 117; **Richard Lovelace,** *Homosexuality and the Church* (Fleming H. Revell, 1978), p. 19.

45 Sherwin Bailey, op. cit., p. 119.

46 Boswell, CSTH, pp. 303ff.

47 Martin Luther, *Lectures on Genesis,* in *Luther's Works,* III, Jaroslav Pelikan, ed. (Concordia Press, 1961), pp. 239, 251–5.

48 Martin Luther as quoted in **Lovelace,** op. cit., p. 19.

49 Joel Harrington, *Reordering Marriage and Society in Reformation Germany* (Cambridge University Press, 1995), pp. 37, 215.

50 John Calvin, *Commentary on Genesis* (Edinburgh: Banner of Truth Trust, 1975), p. 496.

51 John Calvin, *Commentary upon Romans* (Calvin Translation Society, 1849), p. 33.

52 John Calvin, *Commentary upon 1st Corinthians* (Calvin Translation Society, 1848), p. 209.

53 Heinrich Bullinger, *The Decades,* I (Cambridge University Press, 1849), p. 418.

54 Thomas Goodwin, *Works,* X (James Nichol, 1865), p. 320.

55 David Clarkson, *Works,* III (Edinburgh: Banner of Truth Trust, 1985), pp. 231–2.

56 Richard Baxter, *Christian Directory* from *The Practical Works of Richard Baxter,* I (Soli Deo Gloria, 1990), pp. 437,453.

57 Matthew Henry, *Expositions of the Old and New Testaments* (Henry G. Bohn, 1846), Genesis 19:4.

58 Ibid. Judges 19:22–30.

59 Jeremy Taylor, *Holy Living and Holy Dying* (George Bell & Sons, 1898), p. 447.

60 Andrew Fuller, *Works,* III (Sprinkle Publications, 1988), pp. 75, 77.

61 David Greenberg, op. cit., pp. 303–28; **Lawrence Stone,** *The Family, Sex and Marriage* (Wiedenfeld & Nicolson, 1977), pp. 492, 541.

62 Simon Schama, *The Embarrassment of Riches* (Fontana Press, 1988), pp. 601–6.

63 See **Cantarella,** op. cit., p. 152.

64 John Knox and Gerald R. Cragg, *Romans* in *The Interpreter's Bible,* Vol. 9 (Abingdon Press, 1954), p. 402.

65 Karl Barth, *Church Dogmatics,* III.4 (T. & T. Clark, 1961), p. 166.

66 Lovelace, op. cit., pp. 23–24.

67 Helmut Thielicke, *The Ethics of Sex* (Jas. Clarke & Co., 1964), pp. 269ff; **Lovelace,** op. cit., pp. 24–27.

68 Alan Shead, 'Homosexuality and the church: historical survey' in *Theological and Pastoral Responses to Homosexuality,* Explorations 8, B.G. Webb, ed. (Open Book, 1994), pp. 7–8.

69 Norman Pittenger, *Time for Consent—A Christian's Approach to Homosexuality* (SCM 1976), p. 38.

70 J.J. McNeill, *The Church and the Homosexual* (Darton, Longman and Todd, 1977).

71 Letha Scanzoni and Virginia Mollenkott, *Is the Homosexual My Neighbour? Another Christian View* (SCM, 1978); **Virginia Ramey Mollenkott,** *Sensuous Spirituality* (Crossroad, 1992).

72 Pim Pronk, *Against Nature—Types of Moral Argumentation Regarding Homosexuality* (Wm B. Eerdmans, 1993), pp. 322, 324.

73 Shead, op. cit., pp. 18ff.

Just genetics?

Peter Saunders

Introduction

Karoly Maria Benkert coined the term homosexuality in 1869. The prefix 'homo' comes from the Greek word meaning 'same', the opposite of 'hetero' or 'other'. *The Oxford Dictionary* defines homosexuality as 'being sexually attracted only by members of one's own sex', but there is no universally accepted definition among clinicians and behavioural scientists. There is even less agreement as to its cause.

Part of the problem is that not all people are exclusive in their sexual inclinations. There is a spectrum ranging from those who have never had a homosexual thought in their lives, to those who experience nothing else. In the 1940s Alfred Kinsey conducted a major study[1] into sexuality and classified subjects on a continuum from 0 (exclusively heterosexual) to 6 (exclusively homosexual) with grades of bisexuality (attraction to both sexes) in between.

Another difficulty with definitions is that sexual desire may or may not correlate with sexual behaviour. Some people with exclusively same-sex erotic fantasies may never proceed to homosexual activity, and in fact may live in long-term heterosexual relationships. Others with sexual desire only for the opposite sex may, under extreme circumstances (such as in prisons or during wartime), participate in homosexual acts. The term 'sexual orientation' is now commonly used to describe the predominant sexual preference.

Changing perceptions

Medical perceptions of homosexuality have changed. In the nineteenth century it was attributed first to moral degeneracy and later to mental illness. In the early twentieth century it was credited to hormonal imbalance, to psychosocial influences and, more recently, to biological factors. Many now see it simply as a natural variant like handedness or skin colour. As recently as 1967 in the United Kingdom, homosexual behaviour between consenting adults in private was a criminal offence at any age. In

1974 the American Psychiatric Association voted to drop homosexuality from its official list of mental disorders (DSM II) and in 1994 the British Medical Association (BMA) Council joined in calls for the lowering of the age of homosexual consent.

This change in perception rests on the presupposition that homosexual orientation is biologically determined and unchangeable and much of the current literature focuses on the need to help homosexuals embrace their sexuality and cope with discrimination. Some within the American Psychiatric Association are now calling for an official ban on therapy to change the condition (reparative therapy).[2]

Now that homosexuality has attained 'non-pathological status' it is increasingly difficult to ask fundamental questions or to carry out research that challenges the prevailing view. As one commentator has put it, 'this is an area, *par excellence*, where scientific objectivity has little chance of survival'.[3]

The problem is clearly displayed in a 1996 review of the current state of biomedical research on homosexuality. This review concluded that the causes of homosexuality are unknown, that sexual orientation is likely to be influenced by both biological and social features, and that the area should be studied. The review then argued that research into the causes of homosexuality would be unethical and should not therefore occur.[4] Consequently little work has been carried out recently. A 1997 review of the most likely causes of homosexuality concluded that the scientific study of sexual orientation is, at best, still in its infancy.[5]

Vested interests

It is difficult not to bring one's own preconceptions to scientific investigation. The temptation (consciously or unconsciously) is to view the facts selectively in order to prove the rightness of one's own prior convictions. Many researchers are quite open about having an agenda other than the mere pursuit of scientific truth. If sexual orientation is not fixed, then, according to US law at least, homosexuals may not be protected from 'discrimination'.[6] Bailey and Pillard, two of the most prolific medical researchers in the field (and leading advocates for the view that homosexuality is inborn) have commented that 'a biological explanation (of homosexuality) is good news for homosexuals and their advocates'.[7]

Another author has suggested that if homosexuality is a purely biological phenomenon, 'society would do well to re-examine its expectations of those who cannot conform'.[8]

Researchers who have the added motivation of changing public opinion will be guided along certain channels in their work. There are now powerful interests in the scientific community attempting to prove that homosexuality is uniform across time and culture and therefore 'natural', that sexual orientation is established early in life, that it cannot be changed even with 'treatment' and even that homosexuals are in some way genetically superior and therefore favoured in the evolutionary process.[9]

The influence of media and pressure groups

Journalists can also bring their private social agendas to bear by selective and sensational reporting of research findings. Tenuous conjecture is then interpreted to a gullible public as certain conclusion. Gay rights activists have used sympathetic academics and a supportive press to seek minority status for homosexuals and the abolition of all forms of perceived discrimination. Practising homosexuals, they argue, should be given equality in the workforce, in social welfare and in being able to marry and raise (adopted or artificially conceived) children. The strategy, as outlined in books by gay authors, such as *The Homosexualisation of America* and *After the Ball*[10] is as follows: 'divert attention from what homosexuals do, make homosexuality a topic of everyday conversation, portray homosexuals as normal and wholesome in every other way, and portray those who disapprove of homosexual behaviour as motivated by fear, ignorance and hatred'.[11]

It is, of course, quite appropriate for the public to be responsibly informed about scientific discoveries, but twenty-second soundbites cannot do justice to complex controversies, especially when those holding a contrary view are not given the opportunity to respond. 'The first to present his case seems right, till another comes forward and questions him' (Proverbs 18:17).

Balancing word and world

Of course, we have to be careful not to fall into the same trap ourselves, by selectively using scientific findings to bolster our own position. We need to cultivate an open-mindedness which neither gullibly accepts nor quickly rejects new data, but which rather tests the claims of scientists rigorously. The biblical injunction to 'inquire and make search and ask diligently' (Deuteronomy 13:14) is surely relevant here. We can expect that just as the Bible will lead us to question whether we have interpreted the scientific facts correctly, so scientific discoveries may lead us to question whether we have interpreted the Bible correctly. We need to balance revelation and science, the word and the world, in a humble search for the truth—knowing that, properly interpreted, science and the Bible should not contradict each other.

The limitations of science

When it is next announced by the media (as it inevitably will be) that, for instance, scientists have discovered a 'gay gene', or a difference in the brain structure of homosexuals, we should evaluate the evidence for such a claim carefully before jumping to conclusions one way or the other.

First, we need to ask whether the research has been replicated elsewhere. Often other studies will have been published which come to opposite conclusions. If the issue has never been addressed before, we need to wait to see if independent investigators can repeat the study and come to the same conclusions. A classic example of this kind of error was the Kinsey Report.[12] For decades researchers adopted Kinsey's figure of 10% for the incidence of homosexuality in the general population, not realising that this estimate was based on a poorly designed study of a non-randomly selected sample population, 25% of whom were (or had been) prison inmates. The figure stood unchallenged largely by default until quashed by contemporary research. The finding in a recent British sex survey[13] that only 1 in 90 people had had a homosexual partner in the previous year, is much more in keeping with the figure of 1–2% now generally quoted. Research published in 2001 indicated that 2.6% of both men and women reported homosexual partnerships.[14]

Second, we need to look at the response from the rest of the scientific community. Other researchers may examine the findings of the study in question and not agree that they warrant the claims made. When it was announced in 1993 that homosexual orientation had been mapped to a small section of the X chromosome,[15] the media uncritically propagated the news as fact. However, an editorial reviewing the findings that was published shortly afterwards in the British Medical Journal[16] was far more cautious. Not surprisingly this review was not given the same high profile in the popular press.

Third, we need to ask whether there are confounding variables in the study which could be distorting the results. If subjects for a study are not randomly selected from the general population, or if like is not being compared with like, then the results can be skewed. For example, subjects for a key study[17] claiming to prove that homosexuality has a genetic basis were actively recruited through homophile magazines–hardly an unbiased sampling process.

Fourth, we need to ask whether an apparent link between, say, homosexual orientation and brain structure, is a direct effect or not. In other words does the brain difference cause the sexual orientation or vice versa? Or, alternatively, is the observed difference a consequence of some third factor such as the disease process AIDS?

Fifth, we must avoid simplistic solutions to complex problems. As science progresses, it becomes increasingly clear that nature is far more complex than we first imagined. With homosexuality the lack of any real consensus regarding cause should make us suspect that we are not dealing with simple cause and effect.

Nature or Nurture?

Having laid this framework, we now proceed to examine the evidence put forward. What is it that makes one person experience homosexual thoughts while another does not? Is homosexuality something genetic, or is it a result of upbringing? Is it biological or psychosocial? Or, to use biblical terminology, are people 'born that way' or 'made that way by men' (Matthew 19:12)? Furthermore, if nature or nurture (or both) are involved, then what part does personal choice play in a person adopting a homosexual lifestyle?

Opinions on these questions differ widely among leading researchers. Some, like Boston psychiatrist Richard Pillard, conclude that 'homosexual, bisexual and heterosexual orientations are an example of the biologic diversity of human beings, a diversity with a genetic basis'.[18] Others, like

Van Wyk and Geist, contend that 'biologic factors exert at most a predisposing rather than a determining influence'.[19] Still others hold the middle ground. Let us review the evidence.

Nature arguments

Those who advocate a biological cause have argued that homosexuals possess different hormonal mechanisms, brain structure, or genotype. Such biological explanations may not be unrelated, as genes lay the blueprint for hormones which in turn influence body structure. We will look at each in turn.

1. HORMONAL MECHANISMS

Hormones are chemical substances produced in the body which have specific regulatory effects on particular body cells or organs. Male sex hormones, or androgens, are produced by the testis and are responsible for the development of secondary sex characteristics like chest and pubic hair and a deepened voice. Female sex hormones, or estrogens, are produced by the ovary and bring about pubic hair growth and breast development. The release of these sex hormones, and indeed the development of the gonads (testis and ovary) themselves, is in turn regulated by other hormones called gonadotrophins (LH and FSH) produced in the pituitary gland at the base of the brain. These are in turn regulated by a third group of hormones (releasing factors) produced just above the pituitary in a part of the brain called the hypothalamus. A delicate balance is maintained.

At one stage it was thought that homosexuals were hormonally different (e.g. in their circulating levels of reproductive hormones), but this idea was abandoned when sensitive hormone assays became available and accurate measurements could be made.[20] However, the possibility remains that hormones might play a part in the *prenatal development* of the brain, and hence in sexual orientation and behaviour.

Female rats exposed to androgens in early development exhibit 'mounting', a typically male sexual response.[21] By contrast, neonatally castrated male rats exhibit 'lordosis', a sexually receptive back-slouching position characteristic of females.[22] Is the rat brain being hormonally programmed in some way during fetal development? Could the same sort of thing be occurring in humans who later show homosexual tendencies?

There are limits in extrapolating data from these rodent studies and applying them to human beings. First, sexual behaviours in rats are under rigid endocrine (hormonal) control. By contrast, in humans sex is not a reflex but a complex and conscious behaviour. There is no human equivalent for stereotyped 'lordosis' or 'mounting'. Second, human homosexuals engage in both receptive and penetrative intercourse; whereas in this model 'mounting' and 'lordosis' were gender-specific. Third, the prenatal hormone theory fails to explain the complexity and variability of the human sexual response with changes of erotic fantasies, modes of sexual expression, and indeed even sexual orientation over time.

If the prenatal hormone hypothesis were correct, we would expect to find a higher incidence of abnormal gonadal structure or function in homosexuals. We do not. We would also expect to find a higher proportion of homosexuals among patients with disorders involving androgen excess or deficiency. Again, extensive reviews of the literature suggest that this is not the case.[23] For example, there is no evidence that children resulting from hormonally treated pregnancies develop homosexual tendencies.[24]

Some very rare medical conditions, in which the affected person's sexual status is ambiguous, have however been put forward as providing evidence for a hormonal cause of homosexual orientation. One example is testicular feminisation. Affected individuals are genetically male (i.e. they have XY chromosomes) and have testes which are normal but remain in the abdomen. They also have female external genitalia that appear normal. Often these individuals do not come to medical attention until after puberty, when they present with amenorrhea (a failure to menstruate) and infertility. On psychosexual testing they are indistinguishable from heterosexual genetic females in terms of sexual arousal and erotic imagery.[25] However, because they are raised as females (because they look like females), this does not prove that sexual preference is hormonally programmed, rather than environmentally conditioned.

Congenital adrenal hyperplasia is a condition in which genetic females are exposed to excessive levels of androgens produced by the adrenal gland, resulting in masculinised (part-male, part-female) genitalia. The vast majority of women with congenital adrenal hyperplasia develop heterosexual interests and there is no consistent evidence for an increased incidence of lesbianism with this condition. Even if this were shown to be the case, it would be almost impossible to demonstrate that this was due to a hormonal effect on the brain rather than the psychological effect of having masculinised genitalia.

Of course, it needs to be stressed that the vast majority (99%) of homosexual people have no measurable hormonal abnormality. The case for a hormonal cause of homosexuality remains as yet unproven.

2. BRAIN STRUCTURE

Could homosexuality be the result of differences in the structure of the brain? Again, studies in rodents have aroused suspicions. The hypothalamus, situated at the base of the brain, is an important hormone control centre. Within its substance lie 'nuclei', tiny bundles of nerve cells each no bigger than the head of a pin. Because of their minute size they can only be properly examined in an autopsy. In rats one of these nuclei (SDN-POA) is sexually dimorphic—that is, it is a different size in males and females. This finding has fuelled speculation that similar differences may exist in humans—not only between sexes but also between homosexual and heterosexual people. Much current research involves examining microscopic portions of post-mortem brain tissue, in attempts to prove that these variations exist.

In 1984 two scientists named Swaab and Fliers claimed to have found a hypothalamic nucleus that was larger in men than in women.[26] Later, however, they were unable to establish a link between its size and sexual orientation.[27] In 1991 a neurobiologist named LeVay dissected the brains of 35 males and reported that the size of another hypothalamic nucleus (INAH3) in the homosexual men was smaller than its counterpart in heterosexual men and the same size as that of the women.[28] The study was highly publicised, but again there were reasons to be cautious. Firstly, the numbers involved were small. Secondly, most of the homosexual men with abnormal hypothalamuses had died of AIDS. Thirdly, it was not apparent how the anatomical area involved could have had a bearing on sexual behaviour. Fourthly, even if it could have had such a bearing, it would remain to be proven that the structural change was the cause, rather than the result, of the altered sexual orientation. Finally, other researchers have pointed to technical flaws[29] in LeVay's research methodology. A more recent study has corroborated LeVay's reports of sexual dimorphism of INAH3 but provides no support for previous reports of sexual variation in other hypothalamic nuclei.[30]

In addition to the hypothalamus, the commissures (bundles of nerve fibres joining the two sides of the human brain) have been extensively examined. Allen and Gorski, again in a well-publicised study, reported in 1992 that the anterior commissure was smaller in heterosexual men than in homosexual men and heterosexual women.[31] However, there was considerable overlap between the three groups and again the majority of homosexual subjects had AIDS. A review of the data in 2002 found that the results of different studies conflicted, and there was no evidence of this variation.[32]

There have also been claims that the corpus callosum (a much larger commissure) may be female-typical in homosexual men, but the 23 studies reported thus far have yielded conflicting results.[33]

In summary, we have currently uncorroborated reports that three different brain structures may possibly show structural variation with sexual orientation. However, in each study the sample size was small, the possible relation between the structure and sexual preference has not been established, and the confounding effect of AIDS has not been adequately addressed.

3. GENETIC STUDIES

In the human body there are 100 trillion cells, each possessing a nucleus containing more information than an average laptop computer. This information is written on 46 chromosomes, arranged in 23 pairs, with each pair consisting of one chromosome from each parent. The chromosomes are constructed from coils of a ladder-shaped molecule called DNA, which makes up our genes. The genetic language has an alphabet of four letters (bases), and if we were to take the entire amount of information in any one cell nucleus and print it out 1,000 letters to a page it would fill 3,000 books of 1,000 pages each. The letters are grouped together into three-letter words (codons) strung together into sentences (genes). Each of the 30,000 genes in the body carries the instructions for the production of a specific protein. Proteins perform a vast variety of actions—from determining the detailed structure of our organs, to transporting chemical substances from one part of the body to another, to controlling the thousands of chemical reactions that are occurring in our different cells. In so doing, genes govern everything from handedness to eye-colour, from appearance to temperament.

There are about 6,000 known genetic diseases (disorders resulting from spelling mistakes in the genetic language which can be passed on from parents to children), and 21,000 children in the UK are born with one of these diseases each year. These conditions vary widely, however, in their severity, frequency, mode of inheritance and expression. Some are lethal (such as those causing many miscarriages), while others may produce no discernible effects at all. Some (like Down's syndrome) are common, while others are extremely rare. Some (like Huntington's disease), if passed from a parent will be expressed in the next generation, while others (like cystic fibrosis) may skip generations completely or simply create a predisposition for the disorder rather than guaranteeing its occurrence.

Could homosexual orientation have a genetic component? Could it even be entirely genetically programmed?

The possibility of a genetic basis for homosexuality has been recognised ever since Kallman evaluated the twin siblings of homosexuals and found that 100% of identical twins, but only 12% of non-identical (fraternal) twins were also gay.[34] While he used a biased sample (most were mentally ill and institutionalised men), and his results have never been reproduced, there have been further studies attempting to show that homosexuality runs in families. The most famous of these are two studies by Bailey. The first showed that 52% of the identical twins of gay men were also gay, while only 22% of non-identical twins were.[35] The second study gave corresponding figures of 48% and 16% for the twin sisters of gay women.[36]

There are reasons to be cautious about assuming that these observed effects were due to genes rather than upbringing. First, identical twins are more likely to be treated similarly by parents and others, especially if they have similar temperaments. Even within the same family, children are raised in quite different ways. The fact that non-twin brothers are less likely to share a homosexual orientation than non-identical twin brothers suggests that environment plays a large part—because non-identical twins and non-twin siblings share the same proportion of genetic material. Second, neither study drew subjects randomly but recruited them through homosexual-oriented periodicals. This must at the very least introduce the possibility that twins wanting to establish that homosexual orientation is genetic may have been more ready to apply. Was the sampling really unbiased? Third, there has so far been only one small and inconclusive study[37] comparing the sexual orientation of twins who have been reared apart since birth. This variable is, in fact, the best way of ensuring that environmental factors do not confuse the picture. Fourth, even if homosexual orientation is influenced by genetic factors, the presence of a 'gay gene' is not necessarily proven. We may simply be talking about a character trait which makes a child more likely to be treated in a way that might lead to a development of a homosexual orientation. Fifth, the authors' interpretation of their data has been cast into serious doubt by statistical reanalysis that found no difference between the groups.[38] Finally, even if we accept Bailey's results, there is still a large proportion of identical twins (about 50%) who develop different sexual orientations, despite allegedly sharing the same prenatal and family environment.

With the rapid advances in our ability to unravel the genetic code, researchers are now trying to discover where on the 46 chromosomes each of the 30,000 known human genes is located. This international collaborative effort, known as the human genome project, is now well under way, and understandably there are attempts to locate a gene for homosexual orientation. In 1993 Hamer, a geneticist working in the field, claimed to have done just that in a paper published in the journal *Science*. He reported that 33 of 40 homosexual non-twin brothers had homosexual relatives on their mothers' sides with similar DNA markers in a region of the female X chromosome known as Xq28.[39] There was considerable media interest in what came to be known as the 'gay gene' but also, as mentioned, less enthusiasm in the medical press.[40] An article in *Nature* commented, 'Were virtually any other trait involved, the paper would have received little public notice until the results had been independently replicated.'[41] The study sample was small, other researchers have not yet confirmed the results, and there is not as yet any indication of how frequent the Xq28 sequence is in the general population. One researcher who reanalysed Hamer's data stated, 'Using the more appropriate (statistical) test I compared several pairs of relatives ... there is no evidence for a maternal effect ... Until these results are replicated ... they should be viewed with extreme scepticism.'[42] Criticism of this study has continued, and few people now give much weight to its evidence.[43]

In fact no 'gay gene' as such has so far been located, let alone had its component DNA sequenced. Even if such a gene is discovered, this may simply carry the instructions for a character trait rather than homosexual orientation as such. Furthermore, even if a genetic link is established for a small proportion of individuals in one section of the gay community, it does not follow that it underlies or explains all homosexuality in all individuals. We know, for example, that a small proportion of breast cancer, but by no means all, is linked to one particular predisposing gene.

As we have seen, interest has focused on finding a 'gay gene' in other species. Biologists Ward Odenwald and Shang-Ding Zhang at the National Institutes of Health in Bethesda, Maryland, created a storm of media publicity with their claim to have transplanted a gene into fruit flies which produced homosexual behaviour.[44] As it transpired these flies were bisexual rather than homosexual and no lesbian flies were produced. The complexity of the human sexual response, in comparison with the far simpler reflexes in invertebrates, should lead us to beware of hasty conclusions.

Overall there is some evidence in small studies that genes may have some bearing on the later emergence of a homosexual orientation. However, many questions remain. If homosexual preference (as opposed to homosexual behaviour) were truly genetic, why is it not observed in species other than human beings? Why do a large proportion of identical twins vary in their sexual orientation? Why does sexual preference change over time, or with therapy? Masters and Johnson, in a five-year follow-up of 67 exclusively homosexual men and women, reported that 65% achieved successful changes in their sexual orientation after behaviour therapy.[45] This has been confirmed by more recent research.[46] Clearly we are not dealing with a simple causal link.

Genetic factors may play a part in the development of homosexual orientation, but they are not the full story. Terry McGuire, Associate Professor of Biological Sciences at Rutgers University, New Jersey, urges us to be circumspect about alleged research findings:

Any genetic study must use (1) valid and precise measures of individual differences, (2) appropriate methods to ascertain biological relationships, (3) research subjects who have been randomly recruited, (4) appropriate sample sizes and (5) appropriate genetic models to interpret the data ... To date, all studies of the genetic basis of sexual orientation of men and women have failed to meet one or more of the above criteria.[47]

A subsequent study of approximately 3,000 randomly picked people estimated the heritability of male homosexuality in a range of 0.28–0.65.[48]

While we may not ever find a 'gay gene', there is increasing evidence to suggest that personality variants (in particular novelty seeking, harm avoidance and reward dependence) may well be inherited.[49] These could theoretically predispose a person to the development of a homosexual orientation given the right (or wrong) environment. This leads us to evaluate the role of nurture.

Nurture arguments

The pure biological view is that homosexual orientation is programmed in the genes, fashioned by hormones, and displayed in brain structure. The pure psychosocial view is that the environment writes upon the developing child, in the same way that someone might draw lines on a blank sheet of paper. Both embrace a type of determinism. In the first, the individual is the product of the interactions of chemical reactions. In the second, he or she is programmed by social forces.

As with the biological arguments, we will consider nurture arguments under several headings, although it should be obvious that they interrelate. Let us consider, then, the cultural environment, the family environment, the peer group environment, and the moral environment.

1. THE CULTURAL ENVIRONMENT

The cultural view is that sexual conduct is determined by the society in which one grows up. In other words we learn sexuality in much the same way that we learn cultural customs. Whereas biological sex is set at birth, gender-specific behaviour develops in a cultural context. The interplay of tradition, religious belief and political factors lays a framework for acceptable behaviours that become increasingly ingrained until they eventually feel natural.

The evidence for this is the diversity of sexual behaviour across cultures and across history. There are cultures in which homosexual behaviour is so uncommon that there is no word for it in the language.[50] Similarly, homosexuality in the form of long-term relationships between consenting adults did not seem to exist in western culture before the nineteenth century, at least not in any significant frequency.

2. THE FAMILY ENVIRONMENT

Most nurture theories focus on the pattern of the parent-child relationship. Male homosexuals are more likely to emerge from families where the father is disinterested, remote, weak or overly hostile and the mother is the dominant disciplinarian and warmest supporter.[51] In the same way lesbians may result from families where there is a breakdown of the mother-daughter relationship.

This view has been popularised by Elisabeth Moberly, who has come to the conclusion that homosexual orientation is the result of unmet same-sex love needs in childhood.[52] Martin Hallett, director and counsellor at True freedom Trust,[53] a Christian ministry to Christians struggling with homosexuality, has found that the majority of male homosexuals counselled identify very much with this lack of intimate bonding with the father or any other male role model.[54] As a result the heterosexual identity is not established, and the unaffirmed child suffers later, as an adult, from a lack of confidence and fear of failure in heterosexual contacts. He tries to meet those unmet same-sex needs through sexual relationships. When these fail to satisfy, the result may be an even more compulsive and promiscuous lifestyle.

Sara Lawton,[55] a Christian counsellor specialising in lesbianism and sex abuse, similarly sees the root of female homosexuality as an unmet need for mother love which becomes sexualised in the adult. This can be compounded by repressed trauma (e.g. the mother wanted to abort her), adoption, prolonged separation through illness, or sexual abuse.

The parent-child relationship can also be disturbed through death or divorce. Saghir and Robins found that 18% of homosexual men and 35% of lesbians had lost their father by death or divorce by the age of ten. The figures for male and female heterosexuals were 9% and 4% respectively.[56] The vast majority (up to 70%) of homosexual adults describe themselves as having been 'sissies' or 'tomboys' as children.[57] This is despite the fact that most adult homosexuals fit neither the effeminate male nor masculine female stereotype. While a higher percentage of homosexuals than heterosexuals exhibit some degree of gender nonconformity, we cannot generalise to all cases. Heterosexuals can come from situations of poor same-sex bonding, whereas homosexuals can come from families where the parent-child relationships were good.[58]

However, amidst the enthusiasm to find a biological cause, the extensive experience of counsellors and the memories of homosexuals themselves need to be taken into account. Thomas Schmidt, in an excellent, wide-ranging review of the literature, has commented: '… since developmental theory is now out of fashion, homosexuals are either not asked about or no longer "remember" childhood problems. It is certainly suspicious that, to my knowledge, not a single study of early childhood among homosexuals has been conducted since the early 1980s.'[59]

3. THE PEER GROUP ENVIRONMENT

The forming of a homosexual identity takes time. Before adolescence, most people consider themselves heterosexual, and for the majority these thoughts are reinforced by the peer group. However, for the child who doesn't 'fit in'—the masculine female or the non-masculine male—identification with the opposite-sex peer group may prove easier, especially if there is experience of rejection by same-sex peers. The male child in this situation may be socialised as a girl, and vice versa. This can lead to gender confusion in adolescence and later identification with others of the same sex who are suffering from the same feelings of isolation. In this context the acceptance of the homosexual label can bring security, self-understanding, and acceptance at a level which that individual has never experienced before.

Identification with the gay culture, or 'coming out', has many rewards in terms of escaping from conflict, reducing the pain of rejection and providing human contact. In other words just as peer pressure enhances a sense of sexual identity in those who eventually become heterosexual, so peer pressure can similarly reinforce homosexual feelings and behaviour. A network of supportive friends and perhaps a long-term homosexual relationship can be powerful forces driving people into, and keeping them within, the gay community.

Whether heterosexuals can be recruited into homosexuality is a complex issue, but a disproportionate number of male homosexuals were sexually molested as children. Education promoting the idea that homosexuality is just a genetically programmed normal variant will certainly lessen any stigma and make it easier for those with confused gender identity to enter the gay community.

4. THE MORAL ENVIRONMENT

In all societies children grow up with a set of instilled values giving them a sense of right and wrong. The parental environment will, to a large extent, shape the conscience. Children who are seldom punished will quickly cease to feel guilt when they cross boundaries. On the other hand, if standards are arbitrarily or unfairly imposed, or if the parents are not themselves good role models, children may rebel against their consciences.

Personal conscience can thus be underdeveloped through upbringing, or blunted through disuse. These effects will be intensified if the public conscience itself is changing, as it certainly is with regard to homosexuality. When homosexuality was regarded as degeneracy, there were powerful social pressures preventing its expression. Now that one can incur the wrath of the politically correct for suggesting that homosexuality is anything other than a natural variant, the tables have turned.

My own opinion concurs with that of Bancroft: 'It remains difficult, on scientific grounds, to avoid the conclusion that the uniquely human phenomenon of sexual orientation is a consequence of a multifactorial developmental process in which biological factors play a part, but in which psychosocial factors remain crucially important.'[60]

The role of personal choice

Some argue with advocates of a strong nature or nurture model by claiming that sexual orientation is a myth, and that homosexuality is a matter of simple choice. This is understandable. All of us have a sense that, at least in some small way, we are the masters of our own destinies. We are not solely genetic machines any more than we are blank slates on which experience writes. While most authors recognise the possible importance of both nature and nurture, often too little attention has been given to the ways in which these factors interact, or to the role of personal choice.

At some point every practising homosexual makes a choice to indulge in homosexual fantasy, to identify with the gay community, or to have homosexual sex. And regardless of the strength and power of the temptations encouraging that choice, regardless of the biological and psychosocial forces operating in any individual, from a biblical point of view that choice is always wrong. However, we must not make the mistake of ignoring the role of nature and nurture in making those of homosexual orientation what they are. Having a homosexual orientation is not often a matter of choice.

An interactive model

While there will always be those who support one model of causation—be it nature, nurture or choice—above all others, the majority of scholars concede that many factors are involved. Heredity and environment are both important and personal choice is clearly involved too. How these elements interact in any one individual may differ, and this explains why one or more of the biological or psychosocial ingredients may be lacking in any one case.

For example, a boy with a biological predisposition to 'girlish' behaviour is born into a dysfunctional family where the father is remote and the mother smothering. He grows up with little moral training in a society where homosexuality is viewed as a normal variant. He experiments with homosexual behaviour in adolescence and finds companionship and identity through a long-term homosexual relationship at university, before entering the gay subculture in a large city.[61] The process may be interrupted or diverted at any point—if the biological disposition is not there, if the family dynamics or society's attitudes are different, or if a conscious choice is made not to proceed. But the process is complex and multifactorial, different for each individual. This should leave us with a humble and open attitude, willing to learn more from scientific research and the testimony of skilled counsellors and gay people, so that we can come to understand and respond appropriately to the factors involved in any individual case.

What is natural?

Explaining *how* a homosexual orientation may develop, and understanding *why* some individuals are more susceptible than others does not start to answer the question of how people should behave.

There is often an unstated assumption that strong feelings should determine behaviour, whereas this is not in fact accepted in almost any other area of life. We do not believe, for example, that a strong desire to smoke or to drink should be rewarded with the provision of cigarettes or alcohol. Nor do we accept that lust legitimises adultery or that envy sanctions stealing or greed.

Many of the desires we have, if acted upon, lead to damaging not only other human beings but ourselves as well. As the Bible succinctly puts it: 'There is a way that seems right to a man, but its end is the way to death' (Proverbs 14:12), or 'The heart is deceitful above all things and beyond cure' (Jeremiah 17:9, NIV). God calls us to resist evil desires—not to act on them, but rather to obey him with the strength his Spirit gives.

The gay rights lobby presupposes that what comes naturally is good. By contrast the biblical world view is that the whole world, and human beings themselves, are polluted by sin which has affected our bodies (and this must surely include our genes), our minds, our wills and our feelings. Consequently our biology, our thoughts, our choices, and our desires are not what they were intended to be. In the biblical scheme 'natural' (as in Romans 1:27) means not 'what comes naturally' but rather 'what God intended (and intends) us to be'.

Summary

This complex subject has been helpfully reviewed recently by a variety of

Christian authors.[62] But, in fact, not much has changed in the research area in the past few years. While Christians will see both homosexual orientation and behaviour as evidence that we live in a fallen world, we must not retreat into a simplistic analysis that sees homosexual behaviour simply as arbitrary personal choice. The exact means by which sin exerts its effects on societies and individuals is only in part discernible by us as sinful human beings. It should come as no surprise to discover that sin should affect even our genetic code, hormonal functions and body structures. The ageing process itself, for example, is a consequence of sin and yet mediated by these same factors. Why not then a predisposition to homosexual orientation? In the same way, we should not be surprised that our upbringing may have profound effects on our temperaments and personalities. This is not to deny that all of us, homosexual or heterosexual, are sinners by choice. But we are also sinners by nature, both by virtue of living in a fallen world, and by being sinned against by others. Regardless of what may come to be known in the future about the relative contribution of nature, nurture and personal choice to the development of homosexuality, its complete healing will only be found through repentance, faith, forgiveness, regeneration and ultimately resurrection of the body in a new heaven and a new earth.

Notes

1 **A. Kinsey et al,** *Sexual Behaviour in the Human Male* (W.B. Saunders, 1948).

2 **C. Socarides and B. Kauffman,** 'Reparative Therapy' (letter), *American Journal of Psychiatry,* 151 (1994): 157–59.

3 **J. Bancroft,** 'Homosexual Orientation: The Search for a Biological Basis', *British Journal of Psychiatry,* 164 (1994): 437–440.

4 **U. Schuklenk and M. Ristow,** 'The Ethics of Research into the Cause(s) of Homosexuality', *Journal of Homosexuality* 31, no.3 (1996): 5–30.

5 **W. Byne and E. Stein,** 'Ethical Implications of Scientific Research on the Causes of Sexual Orientation', *Health Care Analysis* 5, no.2 (1997): 136–48.

6 **R. Green,** 'The Immutability of (Homo)sexual Orientation: Behavioural Science Implications of a Constitutional (Legal) Analysis', *Journal of Psychiatry and Law* (winter 1988): 537–575.

7 **M. Bailey and R. Pillard,** in 'Opinions and Editorials', *New York Times* (17 December 1991): 19.

8 A. Bell et al, *Sexual Preference: Its development in Men and Women* (Bloomington, Ind.: Indiana University Press, 1981), p. 219.

9 F. Muscarella, 'The Evolution of Homoerotic Behaviour in Humans', *Journal of Homosexuality* 40, no.1 (2000): 51–77. This article supposedly explains why homosexuals have an adaptive advantage.

10 D. Altman, *The Homosexualisation of America* (Boston: Beacon Press, 1982); M. Kirk and H. Madsen, *After the Ball* (New York: Doubleday, 1989).

11 T. Landess, 'Gay Rights in America: The Ultimate PR Campaign', *Rutherford Journal* 3, no. 7 (1994): 3–11.

12 A. Kinsey et al, *op. cit.*

13 A. Johnson et al, *Sexual attitudes and lifestyles* (Blackwell Scientific, 1994), cited by A. Tonks, 'British Sex Survey Shows Popularity of Monogamy', *British Medical Journal*, 308 (1994): 209.

14 A. Johnson et al, 'Sexual Behaviour in Britain: Partnerships, Practices, and HIV Risk Behaviours', *The Lancet* 358 (2001): 1835–42.

15 D. Hamer et al, 'A Linkage between DNA Markers on the X Chromosome and Male Sexual Orientation', *Science* 261 (1993): 321–327.

16 M. Baron, 'Genetic Linkage and Male Homosexual Orientation', *British Medical Journal*, 307, (1993): 337–38.

17 J. Bailey and R. Pillard, 'A Genetic Study of Male Sexual Orientation', *Archives of General Psychiatry* 48 (1991): 1089–1096.

18 R. Pillard and M. Bailey, 'A Biologic Perspective of Heterosexual, Bisexual and Homosexual Behaviour', *Psychiatric Clinics of North America* 18, no.1 (1995): 71–84.

19 P. Van Wyk and C. Geist, 'Psychosocial Development of Heterosexual, Bisexual and Homosexual Behaviour', *Archives of Sexual Behaviour* 13 (1984): 505–544.

20 H. Meyer-Bahlburg, 'Psychoendocrine Research on Sexual Orientation: Current Status and Future Options', *Progress in Brain Research* 61 (1984): 375–398.

21 R. Goy and B. McEwen, *Sexual Differentiation of the Brain* (Cambridge, Mass.: MIT Press, 1980).

22 H. Meyer-Bahlburg, 'Sex Hormones and Male Homosexuality in Comparative Perspective', *Archives of Sexual Behaviour* 6 (1977): 297–325.

23 H. Meyer-Bahlburg, 'Sex Hormones and Female Sexuality: a Critical Examination', *Archives of Sexual Behaviour* 8 (1979): 101–119; W. Byne and B. Parsons, 'Human Sexual Orientation: The Biologic Theories Reappraised', *Archives of General Psychiatry* 50 (1993): 228–239. See also R. Pillard and M. Bailey, *A Biologic Perspective.*

24 See W. Byne and B. Parsons, *op.cit.*

25 J. Money et al, 'Adult Heterosexual Status and Fetal Hormonal Masculinisation', *Psychoneuroendocrinology* 9 (1984): 405–414.

26 D. Swaab and E. Fliers, 'A Sexually Dimorphic Nucleus in the Human Brain', *Science* 228 (1985): 1112–1114.

27 D. Swaab and M. Hoffman, 'Sexual Differentiation of the Human Hypothalamus: Ontogeny of the Sexually Dimorphic Nucleus of the Preoptic Area', *Developmental Brain Research* 44 (1988): 314–318.

28 S. LeVay, 'A Difference in Hypothalamic Structure between Heterosexual and Homosexual Men', *Science*, 253 (1991): 1034–1037. LeVay measured postmortem tissue from three subject groups: women, men who were presumed to be heterosexual, and homosexual men.

29 Cf. **W. Byne and B. Parsons,** op. cit.

30 W. Byne et al, 'The Interstitial Nuclei of the Human Anterior Hypothalamus: An Investigation of Sexual Variation in Volume and Cell Size, Number and Density', *Brain Research* 856, nos. 1–2 (2000): 254–58.

31 L. Allen and R. Gorski, 'Sexual Orientation and the Size of the Anterior Commissure in the Human Brain', *Proceedings of the National Academy of Sciences*, USA, 891 (1992): 7199–7202.

32 M.S. Lasco et al, 'A Lack of Dimorphism of Sex or Sexual Orientation in the Human Anterior Commissure', *Brain Research* 936 (2002): 95–98.

33 Cf. **W. Byne and B. Parsons,** *op.cit.*, 235.

34 F. Kallman, 'Comparative Twin Study of the Genetic Aspects of Homosexuality', *Journal of Nervous and Mental Disease* 115 (1952): 288–298.

35 J. Bailey and R. Pillard, 'A Genetic Study of Male Sexual Orientation', *Archives of General Psychiatry* 48 (1991): 1089–1096.

36 J. Bailey et al, 'Heritable Factors Influence Sexual Orientation in Women', *Archives of General Psychiatry* 50 (1993): 217–223.

37 E. Eckert et al, 'Homosexuality in Monozygotic Twins Reared Apart', *British Journal of Psychiatry* 148 (1986): 421–425.

38 T. McGuire, 'Is Homosexuality Genetic? A Critical Review and Some Suggestions' in *Journal of Homosexuality*, 28, nos.1–2 (1995): 115–145.

39 Cf. **Hamer et al,** A Linkage.

40 Cf. **Baron,** *Genetic Linkage and Male Homosexual Orientation*.

41 M. King, 'Sexual Orientation and the X', *Nature* 364 (1993): 288–289.

42 T. McGuire, *op.cit.*

43 G. Rice et al, 'Male Homosexuality: Absence of Linkage to Microsatellite Markers at Xq28', *Science* 284 (1999): 665–67.

44 L. Thompson, 'Search for a Gay Gene', *Time* (12 June 1995): 52–53.

45 W. Masters and V. Johnson, *Homosexuality in Perspective* (Little, Brown and Co., 1979).

46 R.L. Spitzer, 'Can Some Gay Men and Lesbians Change Their Sexual Orientations? 200 Participants Reporting a Change from Homosexual to Heterosexual Orientation', *Archives of Sexual Behaviour* 32, no.5 (2003): 403–17; discussion 417–72.

47 Cf. T. McGuire, op. cit.

48 K.S. Kendler et al, 'Sexual Orientation in a U.S. National Sample of Twin and Nontwin Sibling Pairs', *American Journal of Psychiatry* 157 (2000): 1843–46.

49 C. Cloninger, 'A Systematic Method for Clinical Description and Classification of Personality Variants', *Archives of General Psychiatry* 44 (1987): 573–588.

50 Cf. J. Bancroft, op. cit., p. 439.

51 A. Bell et al, op. cit., pp. 41–62, 117–134.

52 E. Moberly, 'Homosexuality: Structure and Evaluation', *Theology* 83 (1980): 177–184.

53 www.truefreedomtrust.co.uk

54 M. Hallett, 'Homosexuality', *Nucleus* (January 1994): 14–19.

55 S. Lawton, 'Key Issues in Counselling Lesbians: Counselling those struggling with Homosexuality and Lesbianism—a Christian Approach', Lecture 8 in *Signposts to Wholeness Conference* (True freedom Trust, 1994).

56 M. Saghir and E. Robins, *Male and Female Homosexuality: A Comprehensive Investigation,* (Baltimore: Williams Wilkins, 1973).

57 Cloninger, 'A Systematic Method'.

58 R. Friedman, *Male Homosexuality: A Contemporary Psychoanalytical Perspective* (New Haven: Yale University Press, 1988), pp. 33–48.

59 T. Schmidt, *Straight and Narrow? Compassion and Clarity in the Homosexuality Debate* (Leicester: Inter-Varsity Press, 1995), p. 215.

60 J. Bancroft, op. cit., p. 439.

61 Adapted from T. Schmidt, *Straight and Narrow?*, 51.

62 S. Jones and M. Yarhouse, 'What Causes Homosexuality?' in *Homosexuality: The Use of Scientific Research in the Church's Moral Debate*, pp. 47–91; T. Schmidt, The Great Nature-Nurture Debate in *Straight and Narrow?*, pp. 131–59; P. Saunders, CMF Files 20, *Homosexuality*.

The Bible: sexuality and marriage

Paul Brown

This chapter is divided into two main sections, 'The creation pattern', and 'Living in a fallen world'. Underlying the first section is the recognition that the Bible gives us the pattern for life that our Creator intended. Underlying the second section is the fact that through human disobedience the human condition is far from what it was originally. We are flawed people living in a world that is not the good world it was when it came from the Creator's hand. This is the source of all our trouble.

It is easy to see both of these aspects in our present society and throughout history. On the one hand, people want an ordered society and stable marriages with love and security where children can be brought up with the affectionate care of two parents who are both committed to each other and to their children. Here is a generally recognised pattern of family life that has persisted across the world in all ages. Yet, on the other hand, people also want to be free to express their sexual desires—of almost whatever sort—without any limits being imposed on them from outside, to enter into sexual relationships without the commitment of marriage, and to change their partners if they feel this will be best for them.

It is clear that these desires are actually mutually exclusive and that they represent two fundamentally different viewpoints. The first is that there is a Creator and lawgiver, outside of ourselves, who has given us instructions and rules about how we should live. The second is that we are free as individuals to make up our own rules for behaviour, and that doing what we want to do is the way of freedom and happiness. In the end we all have to choose between these alternatives.

The creation pattern
God's pattern for marriage is given at the very beginning of the Bible in the

creation accounts of Genesis 1 and 2. It is Jesus Christ himself who makes this clear. When asked a question about divorce this was where he took his questioners for an answer. 'Have you not read that he who created them at the beginning made them male and female, and said, "Therefore a man shall leave his father and mother and hold fast to his wife, and the two shall become one flesh"? So they are no longer two but one flesh. What therefore God has joined together, let not man separate' (Matthew 19:4–6). Speaking particularly of Genesis 2:21–25 Gordon Wenham says, 'The story therefore needs to be closely read, for in its often poetic phraseology are expressed some of the Old Testament's fundamental convictions about the nature and purpose of marriage.'[1]

We start, however, in Genesis 1. Verses 27 and 28 read, 'So God created man in his own image, in the image of God he created him; male and female he created them. And God blessed them. And God said to them, "Be fruitful and multiply and fill the earth and subdue it and have dominion over the fish of the sea and over the birds of the heavens and over every living thing that moves on the earth."'

Two features of human beings as created are indicated here. Firstly, they were made in the image of God, a point which is repeated for emphasis. Secondly, God made them male and female. After the image of God, the most significant feature is gender differentiation. They were created as sexual beings: physiologically distinct, with the natural desires and emotions, and psychological differences[2] that belong to male and female. There was not, of course, the slightest tension between being in the image of God and being sexual beings. As male and female God blessed them. Their sexuality, including its expression in all the mutuality of love culminating in sexual intercourse, had his approval and distinct blessing. The first obligation that God laid on human beings at the very beginning was, 'Be fruitful and multiply and fill the earth.'[3] Nothing could underline the naturalness, goodness and centrality of human sexuality more emphatically than the fact that the first obligation God placed upon the people he had made required the expression of their sexuality in intercourse. When God saw everything that he had made, he saw that it was very good (v. 31), and that included the fact and expression of sexuality.

Genesis 2 fills out the picture considerably. Here the creation of the first man and of the first woman is spelled out in detail, complementing the general, overall picture of chapter 1. The first point for comment is the fact that the man was lonely and incomplete by himself (v.19). It is God who acknowledges this, and he who supplies the remedy. God did not make another man to meet Adam's need, he made the first woman. Adam's incompleteness had a sexual dimension and required someone human but different from himself. Wenham comments on the phrase 'a helper fit for him': 'The compound prepositional phrase "matching him", literally, "like opposite him" is found only here. It seems to express the notion of complementarity rather than identity. As Delitzsch (1:140) observes, if identity were meant the more natural phrase would be "like him".'4 So Eve was made for Adam, and Adam finds that Eve supplies the companionship that he lacked. Eve was made from Adam's side to indicate that her purpose was to be his companion, and also to show that the man and the woman belong together. They complement each other, find fulfilment in each other and reach their true potential in partnership together.

Secondly, it was God himself who not only formed Eve from Adam's rib but also 'brought her to the man' (v.22). God her Creator 'gave her away'. The joining of Adam to Eve, and their uniting as one flesh was not simply permitted by God, or even mandated by God. He actively brought it about.

Thirdly, it is clear that the example of Adam and Eve is intended to set a pattern for marriage. This was why Jesus Christ referred to this chapter, quoting verse 24. The relationship established in marriage is one which is to take precedence over the parent-child relationship. It is a close and exclusive relationship: 'a man shall ... hold fast to his wife.' So intimate is its unity that the verse continues, '...and they shall become one flesh.' This undoubtedly includes a reference to sexual union (as Paul insists, 1 Corinthians 6:16); but it almost certainly goes beyond it. The physical union is an expression and symbol of the joining of two persons; in the words of Jesus, 'So they are no longer two but one flesh' (Matthew 19:5). The word translated 'wife' (v.24) is actually 'woman'; it is the 'his' that makes it appropriate to translate 'wife' here and in the next verse. In Hebrew (and in Greek) there is a greater emphasis on gender: 'a man shall ... be joined to his woman.'

We ought not to miss the point that while Genesis 2:24 is a comment made by Moses as the author of Genesis, in Matthew 19:4–5, Jesus ascribes it to him 'who created them at the beginning'. It is not simply a deduction from the uniting of the first man and the first woman; it is God setting a definite pattern.

Fourthly, when God brought the woman to the man Adam broke out in an exclamation of wonder and joy in a couplet which could be called the first love poem.[5] Once again the fact that the man and the woman belong together is stressed. The woman was taken out of man, she is bone of his bone and flesh of his flesh, and now they are joined together again and become one flesh.

Finally, the goodness and innocence of the relationship between the first man and woman are brought out by verse 25: 'And the man and his wife were both naked and they were not ashamed.' There was nothing about their union which was inconsistent with true righteousness nor with the closest fellowship with their Creator. Their mutual nakedness was open and pure.

From this brief survey of Genesis 1 and 2 it is possible to consider some of the practical emphases that emerge.

Sexuality

Any Christian view necessarily involves the idea that God as Creator made humans men and women, but the Genesis account stresses this in a way that might not have been anticipated. Involved in sexuality are strong emotions and desires. The yearning for companionship, the desire for sexual fulfilment, the desire for children and for family life are deeply embedded in the human psyche and are all inter-related so that the satisfaction of only one of these components is inadequate. All the desires that arise from our creation as sexual beings are God-given. They are not to be under-rated or marginalised. We all have to recognise our sexuality and come to terms with it in the context of the life to which we are called to live by God.

Marriage

Old Testament Hebrew does not have words that are the real equivalent of our 'marry', 'marriage'. The most usual term for marry is, literally, 'to take a woman', and this is what is found in Genesis (e.g. 4:19; 6:2; 11:29). We would, perhaps, have been glad if God had spelled out precisely what marriage is, what constitutes it, and the roles, responsibilities and relationships between husbands and wives in a short section in the Bible. However, this is not what God has chosen to do. Genesis 2 presents us with a pattern from which, in the light of the rest of Scripture, we have to draw out implications that apply to life and circumstances today. This passage certainly indicates the central importance of marriage for human beings. The male/female differentiation finds its primary fulfilment in marriage; marriage is the basic, fundamental relationship for human beings made in the image of God.

The picture that emerges here is developed in the rest of the Old Testament and is confirmed in the New Testament. 'The ethical ideal is that sexual activity is to be confined within faithful, heterosexual marriage, normally lifelong, and Jesus is recorded as upholding this in his own teaching (Mark 10:1–12; Matthew 5:31–32; 19:3–9; cf. Luke 16:18; 1 Corinthians 7:10–11).'[6] The joy and fulfilment of marriage are celebrated in a number of passages such as Proverbs 5:15–19; 31:10–31; the Song of Songs and Ephesians 5:25–33. The significance and importance of marriage is also indicated by the way the Old Testament sees the relationship between Israel and the Lord in terms of a marriage covenant (e.g. Jeremiah 2:2; Isaiah 62:4,5). And the New Testament views the relationship between Christ and the church in the same way (Ephesians 5:22–33).

The family

The command of God to 'be fruitful and increase in number' (NIV) implies the family. Once children began to be born the first family came into existence. It is clear that it was God's intention from the beginning that children should be brought up by a man and his wife. The fact that children are conceived by an act of love between parents, together with the fact that God began the human race with a single couple—he could have started with a community if he had wished to—indicate that this is so.

While the Bible makes more of the extended family than is customary among western countries today, this should not be used to undermine the importance of the nuclear family. The human race began with a nuclear family. The commandment, 'Honour your father and your mother' (Exodus 20:12) shows its central importance, an importance which comes to a climax in Ephesians 5:22—6:4. Children are to be brought up within the context of a stable, loving relationship between husband and wife. Nearly everyone recognises the importance of this, though not everyone is prepared to follow out in practice what it demands. Within the family children learn to relate to other people, to recognise authority, to consider the needs of others and the good of the whole family unit. As they grow older they interact more and more with the wider family and other families beyond their own. All this has profound implications for society.

Divine institution

Marriage was instituted by God; this is the whole emphasis of Genesis 1 and 2. It is a gift of God, an expression and evidence of his goodness. It is a good gift, but not one to be tampered with or altered according to the desires of human beings. The divine authority of the Creator lies behind the whole arrangement revealed in Genesis 2:18–25. Marriage is between one man and one woman; it constitutes a unity which takes precedence over every other relationship, a unity which is ordained by God so that Jesus can comment, in the light of this passage, 'What therefore God has joined together, let not man separate' (Matthew 19:6).

Our Lord is highlighting the divine authority that lies behind the marriage pattern of Genesis 2. In days when people believe that sexual ethics are simply the concern of the individual, it needs to be stressed that God sets the standards for sexual behaviour, indeed for all human behaviour both individual and social. The pattern he has given and the laws that support it are authoritative, and human beings are accountable to him for their response to the standards he has set. It is not surprising that unbelievers reject what God has laid down; but those who take their commitment to Scripture seriously are committed both to personal obedience and to bear witness to what God has said.

Singleness

In the light of what has been said so far it is essential to make some reference to singleness. There is no doubt that Genesis presents marriage as the norm for human beings as they were created. The Old Testament takes this for granted; so much so that it has no word for 'bachelor'. Are we to assume that singleness is part of the derangement that has come about as a result of the Fall? There is no hint of this in Scripture and the question is not answered. What we do know is that in the New Testament the single condition is shown to be the will of God for some people (1 Corinthians 7:7), and it is clear that for Christians there can be real spiritual advantages resulting from singleness (1 Corinthians 7:25ff.). Vera Sinton says, 'So the Christian perspective on the biblical material is that, while the first created human beings, Adam and Eve, were a married couple, in the new creation the second Adam, Jesus Christ, was a single man. Singleness and marriage are parallel routes for loving and serving in the world and preparing us for life in the resurrection community.'[7] The example of Jesus himself is particularly significant here.

Singleness is at least part of life for everyone and may be the will of God for an individual for the whole of life. Many of those who marry will spend a significant number of their years as single. In the light of Genesis 2 we can deduce that singleness means that sexuality may not be expressed in intercourse, as that lies at the heart of the marriage unity, 'one flesh'. While the Bible does not say that intercourse constitutes marriage, consummation is an essential element (at least in all normal circumstances). Marriage is, by definition, a one-flesh union between a man and a woman. Refraining from sexual intercourse is obligated on all who are not married. Those who desire same-sex relationships are not being discriminated against in this matter; the same prohibition, difficult though some may find it to bear, lies upon all who are unmarried.

Justification for this approach

This way of approaching the subject· through Genesis 1 and 2 has sometimes been criticised, as for example, by Michael Vasey in his book *Strangers and Friends*. One of his main criticisms is that the 'standard argument' 'does not reflect on the cultural diversity found in human relationships. It imposes on scripture the domestic ideals of the nuclear family—a husband and wife with their children enjoying domestic bliss in protected isolation from wider society.'[8]

This can be answered in various ways. First of all, those advancing the argument never intended 'to reflect on the cultural diversity found in human relationships'. Their concern was to discover what the Bible said about marriage and sexual behaviour. Secondly, there is no reason to suppose that those who use this argument necessarily have an ideal of the nuclear family 'in protected isolation from wider society'.

Thirdly, Vasey actually answers this point himself when he writes, 'These great chapters are intended to provide the backcloth to the whole complex story of the ordering of human society. When the text says, "Therefore a man leaves his father and mother and cleaves to his wife, and they become one flesh" (Genesis 2:24), it is implying not the isolation of a married couple from the wider society but the creation of a new unit within society, as noted in the earlier discussion on polygamy, "one flesh" refers to the creation of a new kinship group (cf. Genesis 29:14).'9 Quite so. It is a society based on a network of relationships broadening out from the first marriage and linked again and again by new marriages. As Calvin says, 'God could himself indeed have covered the earth with a multitude of men; but it was his will that we should proceed from one fountain, in order that our desire of mutual concord might be the greater, and that each might the more freely embrace the other as his own flesh.'10

More importantly, Genesis 1 and 2 and the whole of the Pentateuch were written against the background of the cultural diversity found in the human relationships of the tribes that inhabited Canaan. Their culture embraced sacred prostitution, homosexual activity and bestiality, among many other sins, and God's standards are set out in conscious opposition to such behaviour. They act both as a guide and a warning. The bishops write, 'But from the fact that [Jesus] supports with his own authority the statement in Genesis that in the beginning God created humankind male and female, and uses that as a basis for ethical guidance (Matt.19:3–9; Mark 10:1–12), it is not unreasonable to infer that he regarded heterosexual love as the God-given pattern.'11 Rather, it would be unreasonable to infer anything else.

Living in a fallen world
The creation pattern of Genesis 1 and 3 is followed by the account of the

fall of Adam and Eve into temptation and direct disobedience to God's command. The rest of the Bible shows how far-reaching the effects of that disobedience were (see, for example, Romans 5:12–21). Genesis does not explain its significance theologically, but the beauty of the first two chapters gives way to a very different atmosphere in the latter part of chapter 3, in chapter 4 and then on throughout the book, and the whole Bible. There is no suggestion that the first sin was sexual in any way, but it is clear that the results of the Fall have affected every area of life including the sexual.

The first effect on Adam and Eve was that they felt ashamed of their nakedness. Their sexual difference became a source of embarrassment to them. The relationship between Adam and Eve was also obviously deeply affected. Adam blamed his wife for what had happened and the ominous words of verse 16 announced a tension between the sexes that is only too apparent today: 'Your desire shall be for your husband, and he shall rule over you.'[12] As Genesis unfolds, chapter 4 introduces us to bigamy; chapter 6 to lust; chapter 9 to indecent exposure; chapter 19 to attempted homosexual rape and incest. The Fall, and sin as a principle of evil within human beings, is seen to have profound effects upon sexuality and marriage. The first act of disobedience leads to disobedience to the creation pattern for marriage.

The Bible makes it clear that sin affects every part of human nature and every area of human experience. The effects of sin are physical, psychological and emotional as well as moral and spiritual. Just as the natural creation has been spoilt by the Fall and the curse (Genesis 3:17–19), so also people's bodies have been affected. Genetic disorders, physical disability and hereditary disease all arise from the disorder in the created realm that was introduced as a result of the original human disobedience. People's minds and emotions are also affected; some suffer from learning disabilities, others from inherited tendencies to depression or other psychological disorders. The original goodness of the creation has been lost and there are many tragic situations.

This is an area of great difficulty because in practice it can be impossible to distinguish between what is actually sinful, and what are inherited tendencies or developmental damage suffered during early life. Often all three are intertwined in a person's experience. The old adage, 'Love the sinner but hate his sin' is never more relevant than at this point.

The effects of the Fall are also seen in the sexual realm. There can be deformities affecting the sexual organs. Some people are unable to have children of their own. For several possible reasons some people are sexually attracted to those of the same sex, or perhaps to those of both sexes. Some physically belong to one sex yet emotionally feel they belong to the other, and sometimes go to the extent of changing their sex by operation. It is neither possible nor necessary to consider all the variety of conditions possible, for we live in a greatly disordered world.[13] It is a sinful world with much pain and suffering in which we need to love and help each other. What we must not do is to think that by disregarding God's word we can somehow alleviate the pain and improve the situation. In the long term it will be found that deviating from God's ways is always detrimental, and many have sadly proved this to be true.

Homosexuality in terms of orientation, desire and temptation has to be looked at as one of the effects of the Fall. This is not to single out homosexuals in any particular way. All human beings are deeply affected, and sin has corrupted the hearts and desires of us all: 'None is righteous, no, not one' (Romans 3:10). Romans 1, which speaks of 'dishonourable passions' and 'relations … that are contrary to nature' (v.26), goes on to speak of people becoming 'filled with all manner of unrighteousness' (v.29) and specifies all sorts of other evils which, sadly, are the common heritage of people as they are now.

Two implications

Because humanity is fallen it is an over-simplification for people to say, 'God made me as I am.' No one suffering any disability or conscious of a bias to particular sins should simply accept their condition as one intended and made by God. This is a difficult and sensitive point. What we are as individuals undoubtedly comes about in God's over-ruling providence, yet we cannot put down the fallenness of our humanity or our inner tendencies to sin simply to creation by God. God has brought us into the world as we are and put us into our own circumstances not that we should accept either as good in themselves, but as challenges to faith and obedience, and opportunities to prove his grace and power. One person suffers from debilitating migraines; another from bouts of depression that may include temptations to suicide and involve evil obsessive thoughts; another simply has a violent temper. None of these conditions is good in itself. All involve temptations to be resisted, inner battles to fight, things about ourselves that cause us shame and perhaps near despair. But there is grace in Christ and the power of the Holy Spirit available to those who repent and seek that grace and power in faith.

It is also wrong for anyone to affirm or celebrate a state of affairs brought about by the Fall. It is not a good thing for a person to be born with cystic fibrosis, nor is it a good thing, in itself, for a person to have a homosexual orientation. It is true that both conditions are to be accepted as gifts from God and theatres in which his grace can be displayed. But we cannot celebrate or rejoice in the disorderliness brought about by the Fall, nor in doing anything which deviates from God's will. It is tragic when professed Christians believe that they can.

Life after the Fall

Jesus' use of Genesis 2:24 indicates that God's original pattern for marriage still remains valid after the Fall. Prior to the Fall Adam and Eve spontaneously and gladly lived according to that pattern; afterwards things were to be very different. Although basic standards of right and wrong are built in to the consciousness of human beings (Romans 2:14,15), God gave his law in order to make his will for human behaviour explicit. So in the ten commandments marriage is protected by the seventh commandment, 'You shall not commit adultery,' and also the tenth, 'You shall not covet your neighbour's wife' (Exodus 20:14, 17). There are, of course, many other commands concerning marriage and sexual behaviour and both Testaments bear witness to God's displeasure at the different forms of sexual sin that are to be found (see, for example, Ephesians 5:3–6; Galatians 5:19; 1 Corinthians 6:9–20).

Christians are sometimes accused of getting things out of proportion in their attitude to sexual misdemeanours. It is true that it would be wrong to overlook the seriousness of many other evils: covetousness, idolatry, hypocrisy and so on. Nevertheless, marriage has such a crucial place in human life and in the welfare of society that actions which undermine it or which tend to destroy it are very serious. What we have seen earlier of the place God has given to marriage only underlines this. If we think of our own society, irresponsible sexual behaviour underlies the vast majority of our social problems.

God's toleration of departures from his pattern

Though God did not approve of people departing from the creation pattern for marriage, it is clear that in the Old Testament God tolerated this in two respects. First, God tolerated polygamy. Even within the line of the covenant people—even among some of the most godly men of faith—polygamy is found. It is not explicitly condemned, though its disastrous results are exhibited, especially, for example, in the stories of Jacob and David. Secondly, God also tolerated divorce. This was permitted and regulated under the Mosaic legislation, even though it contradicts God's original intention. As Jesus forcefully put it, 'what therefore God has joined together, let not man separate' (Matthew 19:6).

In view of this toleration of polygamy and divorce, it is striking that there is no such toleration of homosexual relationships. Rather, homosexual acts are strongly condemned in the Mosaic law, and there are no examples of homosexual relationships among godly people in the Bible. Those who wish to see a sexual or erotic element in the relationship between David and Jonathan are introducing something that is not there in the text. The idea that because it was a particularly close and deep friendship, a love described as 'extraordinary, surpassing the love of women', it must therefore have been sexual begs the question. Such words could as easily mean that it was of a completely different nature from that of a sexual relationship.

Perhaps the example of David and Jonathan ought to be considered a little further because it is really the only place in the Bible where it is even possible to try and see a homosexual relationship. Both David and Jonathan were married and had children, and David, the one who speaks so movingly of the depth of their love and friendship, clearly had strong heterosexual desires. Vasey accepts that 'there is no suggestion here of a genital relationship between the two men'.[14] If there had been, this would, of course, have been an extra-marital homosexual relationship, something no Christian could argue for.

A further point can be added. The writer of 2 Samuel exposes quite clearly David's adultery with Bathsheba, and God's discipline both in the death of the child and the longer-term consequences in his family (2 Samuel 11–12; note 12:10–14). In the light of this, it is hardly likely that a writer from the Israelite prophetic tradition, with a background formed from passages like Leviticus 18:22; 20:13, would simply pass over a sexual relationship between David and Jonathan if he knew that is what it was. But if *he* didn't know that it was, how can anyone now decide that it was, when we only have his account to refer to? The close same-sex friendship revealed in this story certainly points to the value of such friendships. However, the atmosphere of sexual innuendo in which we now live increasingly means that there is a fear of friendships like this and contributes both to the loneliness of singles and to the withdrawal of married couples into each other and the family.

It is worth diverging a little more from the main theme to notice the strong emphasis on friendship that there is in Scripture. Think not only of verses like Proverbs 17:17; 18:24; 27:6,9–10, but of examples like Ruth and Naomi (Ruth 1:16–18; 2:11–12; 4:15) and Jesus and John (John 13:23). David seems to have made close friends easily, not only with Jonathan, but with Hiram (1 Kings 5:1), Ahithophel (2 Samuel 15:31; Psalm 41:9; 55:20–21), Hushai (2 Samuel 15:37; 16:16), and Barzillai (2 Samuel 17:27–29; 19:31–39). There must surely have developed deep bonds of friendship between Moses and Joshua, Elijah and Elisha, and between Paul and several of his colleagues, Barnabas, Silas and Timothy. It is striking that Abraham is picked out as the 'friend of God', and that Jesus emphasises the closeness of his relationship with his disciples by calling them 'friends' (John 15:13–15). True friendship is a Christian virtue and especially necessary for those who are single (see 2 Timothy 1:16–18). Honest, deep friendship, provided it does not lead to over-dependence on one side, can be of great support to those struggling with their sexuality.

Forgiveness and restoration

Against the background of the Fall and consequent human sin comes the incarnation of the Son of God and his saving life and death. He has come 'to save his people from their sins'. All sexual sins and deviations from God's pattern for sexuality can be forgiven through the sacrificial death of Christ, and are forgiven when repentance and faith in Jesus take place. John 8 records Jesus' attitude towards a woman caught in the very act of adultery. His words are striking: 'Neither do I condemn you; go, and from now on sin no more' (John 8:11). We cannot assume that at this point the woman had repented—this is what Jesus is urging her to do. There is tender compassion on the part of Christ, but also a clear instruction that the woman must turn from her sin. He still has such an attitude of combined compassion and faithfulness to those who fall into all kinds of sins. It is this attitude that his followers must also exemplify.

The power of the Holy Spirit

The gospel does not simply offer forgiveness; there is also the promised gift of the Holy Spirit (Acts 2:38). In 1 Corinthians 6:9–11 Paul says, 'Do you not know that the unrighteous will not inherit the kingdom of God? Do not be deceived: neither the sexually immoral, nor idolaters, nor adulterers, nor men who practise homosexuality, nor thieves, nor the greedy, nor drunkards, nor revilers, nor swindlers will inherit the kingdom of God. And such were some of you. But you were washed, you were sanctified, you were justified in the name of the Lord Jesus and by the Spirit of our God.' It is the last words that are important for our purpose here. Over against what the New Testament calls unclean, or evil, spirits and also the lusts and passions of our fallen nature (see, for example, Ephesians 2:3), there is the Holy Spirit. Not only is he the agent of the new birth in the experience of conversion (John 3:1–8), but as a person he takes up residence in and control of every Christian. He is a power for holiness, goodness and right living according to the will of God. Unfortunately his power and inward working are too often overlooked or undervalued in these days.

For the New Testament, a Christian life is a life lived by the new power of the Spirit. This does not mean that all evil desires are simply eradicated from our hearts, nor that temptations are not sometimes very powerful; it is not a guarantee of an easy or painless life. It does ensure grace and strength to resist temptation, and enables progressive growth in likeness to Jesus.

Single people, those who have been widowed or divorced, those who are attracted to someone who is married, or being married are attracted to another person, or who are attracted to someone of the same sex, may have fierce battles with desire and temptation. But the Holy Spirit is more powerful and there is both the hope of victory and also forgiveness and restoration for those who fall.

Sanctification by the Spirit

It is fascinating to notice in Galatians 5:23 that 'the fruit of the Spirit' includes 'self-control'. This indicates that while it is the Spirit who produces his fruit in Christian lives, part of that is the ability to exercise self-control. In other words the Christian is not passive as the Spirit produces his fruit, but rather intensely active. Earlier Paul had listed the 'works of the flesh' (vs 19–21). In order to desist from these evils, and resist the temptations they present, the Christian needs self-control. Another similar verse of like importance is Romans 8:13—'If by the Spirit you put to death the deeds of the body, you will live' (see also Colossians 3:5ff, and compare the words of Jesus in Matthew 5:29–30). The work of the Spirit enables Christians to put to death, to nip in the bud, temptations and desires for sinful expressions of bodily appetites.

Jesus himself had already made it clear that to follow him involves self-denial: 'If anyone would come after me, let him deny himself and take up his cross and follow me' (Mark 8:34). Self-denial, self-control and attempts to kill off unholy and unclean desires are entirely against the spirit of the age. They are often looked on as actually harmful, especially when it comes to sexual desire. The emphasis of the present outlook is on expressing yourself and doing what you want to do. In this respect Christianity is profoundly counter-cultural. In a fallen world the life of faith, motivated and empowered by the Holy Spirit, means saying, 'No!' to ungodliness and worldly lusts, and living soberly, righteously and godly in the present age (Titus 2:12).

Final observations

Firstly, the Bible picture is quite clear. Sexual intercourse belongs to marriage, and marriage is between a man and a woman. Homosexuality is but one part of a spectrum of disordered sexuality. This means there is no case for isolating homosexual relationships and treating them separately or differently from heterosexual relationships. Homosexuals ask Christians to treat them as a special case and to apply to them standards that do not apply to all people created by God. This cannot be the right way forward.

Anne Atkins writes, 'A Christian I know, whose sexual feelings are entirely directed towards men (and who lives a life of chastity) tells only close friends about his homosexual orientation. "I'm more than just one aspect of myself," he says.'[15] The fact is all people struggle with desires that could get out of hand, and with temptation. Today homosexuals want to set themselves apart as a specific group in society, though one which is fully accepted by society. Those who accept biblical standards will not set themselves apart. They will be free to relate widely with persons of both sexes, to make close friendships and to be involved in church and society. This may well be difficult for them, just as it may for single heterosexual people to live a life of chastity. Many struggle with sexual temptation, and find help from wise counsel and support. All of us need compassion, understanding and care; all at times need rebuke and warning; all of us are tempted to justify and legitimise what we want to do, and to make ourselves special cases to whom the normal rules do not apply.

Secondly, marriage prior to the Fall would have been joyful, harmonious and fulfilling. Perhaps Milton, who so beautifully pictures the mutual joy of Adam and Eve, is not far wrong when he imagines Satan's envy and hatred as evoked by their nuptial bliss:

Live while ye may,
Yet happie pair; enjoy, till I return,
Short pleasures; for long woes are to succeed![16]

Long woes!—is the picture in Genesis now just an unattainable ideal? Do we have to make the best of the situation accepting that fornication, adultery and homosexual relationships are here to stay? From one point of view we do, for these things will certainly continue until the time of Christ's return. However, not only does God's common grace mean that there are many lasting, happy marriages and people living fulfilled single lives, but

God's saving grace gives forgiveness and enables a new start to be made. The new birth and a relationship with Jesus Christ affects and changes every area of life. On the other hand immoral acts and an immoral lifestyle, though forgivable, bring the judgement of God upon people. This is what gives urgency to Paul's words in 1 Corinthians 6: 'Do you not know that the unrighteous will not inherit the kingdom of God? Do not be deceived: neither the sexually immoral, nor idolaters, nor men who practise homosexuality, nor thieves, nor the greedy, nor drunkards, nor revilers, nor swindlers will inherit the kingdom of God' (vv.9–10).

Those who plead for civil partnership as a type of homosexual 'marriage' underestimate what the Bible teaches about marriage. For true bonding and the intimate companionship and unity which are at the heart of marriage, God made a man and a woman and brought them together. The unity of marriage is only possible between those for whom God designed it. The evidence suggests the reality of this. As the Report of the Free Church of Scotland for 1996 says: 'The high incidence of promiscuity among homosexuals, many times higher than among heterosexuals, surely indicates the extreme difficulty, the impossibility almost, of establishing a faithful, stable, homosexual relationship, which indicates in turn that homosexuals do not "fit together" emotionally or domestically.'[17]

Moreover, homosexual 'marriages' are relationships which in themselves cannot issue in children and family life. The fulfilment open to most heterosexual couples is closed to homosexuals in the nature of the case. Christians cannot but be distressed at seeing people taking a route which can never result in the natural outcome of sexual relations, and which is likely to be inherently unstable and unfulfilling.[18]

Thirdly, Christians have not always been very good at understanding or coping with sexuality. Even in New Testament times trends both to sexual denial (1 Corinthians 7:1–9) and to sexual licence (Revelation 2:14–15; 20–23; 2 Peter 2:13,14) are seen. It has never been easy to live in a world where God's standards are known in the conscience (Romans 2:14–15) but where sin warps and drives the natural appetites (cf. Ephesians 4:17–19). Even more so is it difficult today when the media have such a powerful influence throughout society. Young people are particularly exposed, both to the media and peer pressure.

It is important for churches to give clear and practical teaching, and especially for their members to model biblical attitudes to sexuality. This is necessary for the guidance of young people, for the churches to act as salt and light in the world, and for the glory of God. This is not just a vocation for married couples with young children, but for single people, for older couples and for those who are widowed. We have to learn to accept our gender, to recognise the power, importance and essential goodness of sexuality, to submit to the divine institution of marriage as the place for sexual union, and to resist pressure from within and without to compromise God's standards. While doing this we are to develop a whole range of friendships and relationships with people of both sexes, for mutual enrichment and Christian testimony in a world of people, who, though fallen, are yet made by God and retain aspects and vestiges of his image.

This will not be easy. It requires grace from God, and is likely to include falls, sins and the need for forgiveness and restoration on the way. Yet it is God's way and it is good. The goal is not happy marriages. The goal is the glory of God as married and single prove and demonstrate that the will of God is good, acceptable and perfect; that a lifestyle governed by his will in Scripture is beautiful and productive of good for all who are touched by it. That it is also deeply joyful and fulfilling is a bonus.

Notes

1 **Gordon J. Wenham**, *Genesis 1–15*, Word Biblical Commentary (Word Inc., UK edition, 1991), p. 69.

2 See, for example, chapters 10 and 11 'You're a man, aren't you?' and 'Women are different!' in *Men, Women and Authority*, **Brian Edwards, ed.** (Epsom: Day One, 1996).

3 I left out the final words 'and subdue it' because I wanted to focus directly upon procreation. However, **Christopher Ash** in his book *Marriage: Sex in the service of God* (Leicester: IVP, 2003), emphasises that human beings were made male and female for the fulfilment of the task of exercising dominion over the created order. His discussion is illuminating and persuasive and adds another dimension to the argument.

4 **Gordon J. Wenham**, *op. cit.*, p. 68.

5 Ibid. 'In ecstasy man bursts into poetry on meeting his perfect helpmeet.' See also his

discussion on p. 70. **John Milton** in *Paradise Lost*, Book VIII, lines 484–490 has Adam saying, on seeing Eve:

On she came,

Led by her Heavenly Maker, though unseen,

And guided by his voice, nor uninformed

Of nuptial sanctity and marriage rites.

Grace was in all her steps, Heaven in her eye,

In every gesture dignity and love.

I, overjoyed, could not forbear aloud …

6 *Issues in Human Sexuality,* A Statement by the House of Bishops of the General Synod of the Church of England, December 1991 (Church House Publishing, 2nd impression 1993); 2.13; p. 10.

7 **V.M. Sinton**, 'Singleness' in *New Dictionary of Christian Ethics and Pastoral Theology*, **David J. Atkinson and David H. Field,** eds (Leicester: IVP, 1995), p. 79.

8 **Michael Vasey**, *Strangers and Friends: A new exploration of homosexuality and the Bible* (Hodder and Stoughton, 1995), p. 115.

9 Ibid. pp.115–116. On 'one flesh' see also Wenham, *op.cit.*, p. 71. Although I believe 'one flesh' refers in the first place to physical intercourse because of Paul's use of the phrase in 1 Corinthians 6:16, I accept the implication of a new kinship group—the family—which this brings about.

10 **John Calvin**, *Genesis*, (reprint: London: Banner of Truth Trust, 1965), p. 97.

11 *Issues in Human Sexuality*; 2.17, pp. 12–13.

12 **Gordon J. Wenham**, op. cit., pp. 81–82; particularly his comments on Susan Foh's interpretation of 'desire'—'a desire to dominate her husband'.

13 See, for example, the article on 'Transsexualism' by **E.R. Moberly** in *New Dictionary of Christian Ethics and Pastoral Theology*, pp. 863–864.

14 **Michael Vasey**, *op. cit.*, p. 121.

15 **Anne Atkins**, 'Sodom and Gomorrah and Southwark', *Daily Telegraph*, 15 November 1996.

16 **John Milton**, *Paradise Lost*, Book IV, lines 533–535.

17 Report to the General Assembly of the Free Church of Scotland, 1996, (E) Homosexuality, p. 53.

18 See also the quote from Thomas Schmidt in its context in *what some of you were*, **Christopher Keane, ed.** (Matthias Media, 2001), pp. 128–130; **T. Schmidt**, *Straight and Narrow?* (Leicester: IVP, 1995), p. 127.

The Bible: homosexual practice

Paul Brown

What does the Bible actually say about homosexual practice? This chapter examines the relevant passages. The over-riding intention is to try and set out as clearly and honestly as possible what these passages are saying. Where the meaning of a passage is disputed there will be some interaction with differing views, but the main aim is to attempt an honest, objective assessment of the passages concerned. This may sound naïve: do we not all approach the Bible from within our own interpretive circle, with our own expectations and preferences? Yes we do, but that does not mean that the Bible itself does not have something to say to us. The goal is always to let the Bible speak for itself.

There are many, of course, who think that what the Bible says is irrelevant in the twenty-first century anyway. You sometimes hear politicians objecting to morality being based on 'ancient texts', by which they probably mean the Bible and the Qur'an. Why modern texts should necessarily be preferable to ancient texts is not clear. The chaotic state of sexual morality in modern Britain might suggest that the wisdom of the ages has something to say which is being missed by the ethicists and role models of today.

This book, however, is based on the contention that the Bible is the word of God. This does not simply mean that the Bible claims to be true; it goes far beyond that. It means that the Bible is the active voice of the living God speaking through its writers by the Holy Spirit. Just as it was the word of God that called the universe into existence, so it is by the word of God—proclaimed, written, and the written word preached—that the church has been called into existence and is growing throughout the world. It is true, of course, that the church bears the smudge of fallen humanity. Any investigating officer who looked at the church over history and in the present day would report, 'Blundering sinners have been at work here.' But in spite of that, the existence of the church, and all the good it has done over the centuries, and the joy and hope it has brought to its members, have all come through the word of God. 'The words of the Bible are not simply carriers of information but *means of transformation*.'[1] It is not just the existence of the church that bears this out. The conversion of individuals tells the same tale. In this connection it is worth looking at chapter 7 and seeing the role of the Bible in the story recounted there.

The present chapter concentrates on eight passages in the Bible, four from each Testament. It is important to remember that they come in the context of marriage and singleness as described in the previous chapter. They also come in the context of a gospel that offers forgiveness, new life and new power to live a life pleasing to God. David Petersen has made the important point that they come in the context of holiness. Speaking of the current debate within the Church of England he says:

> But the language of holiness is rarely heard. This is remarkable since holiness is the theological context and motivation for the teaching of the Mosaic law about sexual behaviour (Lev. 18:1–30; 20:7–27). Holiness is similarly the basis of Paul's appeal for distinctive sexual behaviour in several key passages (e.g. 1 Thess. 4:1–8; 1 Cor. 6:9–20; 2 Cor. 6:14—7:2) … in terms of biblical theology it is holiness—rather than justice, love, tolerance, unity or personal fulfilment—that should be our first consideration.[2]

It is important to note that these passages are divided between the Old and New Testament. Sometimes there is an undue concentration on the Old Testament references—for example, a long correspondence in the letters page of the Lancaster *Citizen* focused almost entirely on Old Testament references, one side ridiculing them, the other rather ineffectively trying to explain them. If there were no New Testament references then our understanding of those that occur in the Old would be problematic, but there is a consistency between the two Testaments.

Genesis 19:1–11

The two angels came to Sodom in the evening, and Lot was sitting in the gate of Sodom. When Lot saw them, he rose to meet them and bowed himself with his face to the earth and said, 'My lords, please turn aside to your servant's house and spend the night and wash your feet. Then you may rise up early and go on your way.' They said, 'No; we will spend the night in the town square.' But he pressed them strongly; so they turned aside to him and entered his house. And he made them a feast and baked unleavened bread, and they ate.

But before they lay down, the men of the city, the men of Sodom, both young and old, all the people to the last man, surrounded the house. And they called to Lot, 'Where are the men who came to you tonight? Bring them out to us, that we may know them.' Lot went out to the men at the entrance, shut the door after him, and said, 'I beg you, my brothers, do not act so wickedly. Behold, I have two daughters who have not known any man. Let me bring them out to you, and do to them as you please. Only do nothing to these men, for they have come under the shelter of my roof.' But they said, 'Stand back!' And they said, 'This fellow came to sojourn, and he has become the judge! Now we will deal worse with you than with them.' Then they pressed hard against the man Lot, and drew near to break the door down. But the men reached out their hands and brought Lot into the house with them and shut the door. And they struck with blindness the men who were at the entrance of the house, both small and great, so that they wore themselves out groping for the door.

Before looking at this passage in any detail it is useful to consider the background. Sodom is first mentioned in Genesis 13:10–13 which includes this ominous note, 'Now the men of Sodom were wicked, great sinners against the LORD.' It is clear that this indicates that there was a far greater degree of evil in Sodom and the cities associated with it than was general in the land of Canaan. In Genesis 15:18 God speaks to Abraham of his descendants, 'And they shall come back here in the fourth generation, for the iniquity of the Amorites is not yet complete.' Four generations here seem to equate with the four hundred years of verse 13. What God is promising is this: after four hundred years of sojourn in Egypt the people of Israel will return to Canaan, the land of promise, to capture it. By that time the sins of the tribes in the land will have reached such a pitch that the assault by the Israelites will be God's judgement upon them. As Moses explained to the people of Israel, 'Do not say in your heart, after the LORD your God has thrust them out before you, "It is because of my righteousness that the LORD has brought me in to possess this land," whereas it is because of the wickedness of these nations that the LORD is driving them out before you' (Deuteronomy 9:4). If four hundred years were needed before judgement was to fall on the rest of Canaan it suggests a process of increasing evil-doing had been going on for a long time, or at a very great rate, in Sodom.

The immediate context, Genesis 18, shows God telling Abraham what he intends to do (v.17), though what this will be is not explicitly stated. However, before any judgement falls, God says: 'Because the outcry against Sodom and Gomorrah is great and their sin very grave, I will go down to see whether they have done altogether according to the outcry that has come to me. And if not, I will know' (vv.20–21). Presumably this was intended to reassure Abraham of God's absolute justice and it serves to remind us that when God judges it is based on a comprehensive knowledge of every relevant factor. So it was that the two angels—though it is clear that they looked like men (18:2,18,22)—went down to Sodom on a fact-finding mission (19:1). Lot, coming across them in the town square and knowing the character of the men of Sodom, urged them to accept his hospitality and spend the night in his house. Before they had time to settle down to sleep the men of Sodom came and surrounded the house (v.4).

Verse 5 tells us what they said: 'Where are the men who came to you tonight? Bring them out to us, that we may know them.' It is clear from the offer Lot made of his daughters—'I have two daughters who have not known any man' (v.8)—that 'know' is being used of sexual intercourse. This simply repeats the use of the word 'know' in Genesis 4:1, 'Now Adam knew Eve his wife, and she conceived and bore Cain.' This means that it is homosexual intercourse which is in view in this passage, and hence its relevance to the present discussion. A number of considerations immediately arise.

Firstly, it is obvious that it is homosexual rape which was intended. There is menace in the words of the men of Sodom, 'Where are the men who came to you tonight? Bring them out ...' (v.5), and violent means are adopted to get their way, 'Then they pressed hard against the man Lot, and drew near to break the door down' (v.9). In Genesis 6 violence is particularly mentioned as the cause for God's judgement (cf. Jonah 3:8) and the violence indicated here may be significant. Wenham notes that in some places in the ancient world homosexual rape 'was used as a demeaning punishment for prisoners of war'[3] so it is possible that they intended to humiliate the men who had entered their town.

Secondly, it is stressed that the whole male population was involved in this, 'the men of Sodom, both young and old, all the people to the last man' (v.4). This is a scene of terrible degradation; even the old are included in this attempt at gang rape. From our viewpoint this means it is scarcely possible to imagine that every male was homosexual in orientation. Here are people who are slaves to sexual desire who either deliberately want to humiliate the visitors or else desire sexual experiences beyond the normal. Perhaps when sexual licence becomes completely unfettered that is where things can end up. As what was intended here was rape by all the men of Sodom, it is regrettable that homosexual behaviour *per se* was ever given the name sodomy, and it is a good thing that it has largely dropped out of use.

Thirdly, while it is very difficult to understand how Lot could bring himself to say, 'Behold, I have two daughters who have not known any man. Let me bring them out to you, and do to them as you please. Only do nothing to these men, for they have come under the shelter of my roof' (v.8), we do need to consider the implications of his words. The last sentence indicates the importance he attached to having given hospitality, and hence protection, to the men. Actually hospitality is very important in this passage, but it would take us away from our theme to consider it in any detail. Undoubtedly the men of Sodom were violating hospitality codes but it is the way in which they were doing so which is important for our purpose. They would have violated them by taking the men from Lot's house and expelling them from the city, but the way described here is one of the most degrading imaginable.

But Lot's words also seem to indicate 'that it would be better that they satisfy their uncontrollable sexual cravings through natural acts than by grossly unnatural excess'.[4] Lot had said, 'I beg you, my brothers, do not act so wickedly,' which clearly implies that he thought violating the men would be worse than violating his daughters. Moreover, the fact that the men of Sodom rejected Lot's offer and turned on him (v.9) shows that it was homosexual activity that they were bent on. It is difficult to suppress the thought that it was an aggravation of their sin that this was homosexual lust rather than heterosexual lust.

Fourthly, it has sometimes been pointed out that other passages speak of other sins that the people of Sodom were guilty of committing (e.g. Ezekiel 16:49–50). This is true but irrelevant. No one ever supposed that the people of Sodom were models of decency and uprightness apart from their propensity to sexual lust. Nor should we think that Sodom, Gomorrah and the surrounding towns were destroyed simply because of the men of Sodom's behaviour recorded in Genesis 19. What this chapter shows is an example of the depravity that had become commonplace in Sodom; it confirms what God had already said, 'Their sin is very grave' (Genesis 18:20). Of course, this does not lessen the gravity of what happened on this occasion, nor does it deny that this was the sin that finally determined that judgement must fall, but it sets it in the context of the great ungodliness and wickedness of those cities.

Fifthly, this is the first mention of homosexual behaviour in the Bible and it is to this passage that the last mention, Jude 7, refers: 'In a similar way, Sodom and Gomorrah and the surrounding towns gave themselves up to sexual immorality and perversion. They serve as an example of those who suffer the punishment of eternal fire' (NIV). This is clearly a very serious warning. In the first instance it is addressed to those who have secretly come in among Christian believers and 'change the grace of our God into a licence for immorality and deny Jesus Christ our only Sovereign and Lord'.

It would be valuable first of all to attempt a more literal translation: 'As Sodom and Gomorrah and the cities around them in similar manner to these committed sexual immorality and went away from after other flesh.' It is likely that the words 'to these' refer to Sodom and Gomorrah; the cities around them behaved in a similar manner and suffered a similar fate. The verb translated 'went away from' usually has that meaning and together with the phrase 'after other flesh' suggests a turning from what was natural or usual to something other. This is reminiscent of Romans 1:26–27. The key words are 'other flesh', sometimes translated 'strange flesh'. In view of what we are told in Genesis 19 this can only be a reference to homosexual intercourse. The Greek word 'other' is *heteros,* which indicates that in biblical terms to desire sexual relations with the same sex is actually 'other', other than the natural created order. (A more biblical terminology might use the words 'orthosexual' and 'heterosexual' in place of our 'heterosexual' and 'homosexual'!)

One other comment on Sodom seems in order. Our Lord Jesus Christ also referred to it: 'And you, Capernaum, will you be exalted to heaven? You will be brought down to Hades. For if the mighty works done in you had been done in Sodom, it would have remained until this day. But I tell you that it will be more tolerable on the day of judgment for the land of Sodom than for you' (Matthew 11:23–24). Hardness of heart in the face of overwhelming evidence for who Jesus is, and rejecting gospel privileges and opportunities are worse sins than the sins of Sodom.

Leviticus 18:21–23; 20:13

You shall not give any of your children to offer them to Molech and so profane the name of your God: I am the LORD. You shall not lie with a male as with a woman; it is an abomination. And you shall not lie with any animal and so make yourself unclean with it, neither shall any woman give herself to an animal to lie with it: it is perversion.

If a man lies with a male as with a woman, both of them have committed an abomination; they shall surely be put to death, their blood is upon them.

The first passage is one in which a number of sexual relationships are prohibited; the second passage prescribes the penalties for disobedience. Both passages come in a context in which the people of Israel are strongly urged not to follow the practices that have been prevalent in the land of Canaan: 'Do not make yourself unclean by any of these things, for by all these the nations I am driving out before you have become unclean, and the land became unclean, so that I punished its iniquity and the land vomited out its inhabitants. But you shall keep my statutes and my rules and do none of these abominations ...' (18:24–26). God's people are to be different from the pagans that previously occupied the land. This is a reminder that both here and in the New Testament the prohibition on homosexual acts is distinctly counter-cultural. That it should be so in our own day is nothing new.

Both passages refer to extended lists of possible relationships that are prohibited. In nearly every case this is because it would mean marrying a close relative. Without examining the lists in detail, two general points can be made. Firstly, there is a real difference here between the outlook of the Bible and the modern attitude. In the Bible, as in many societies still today, there is a strong emphasis on kinship; on family, clan and tribe. For us the individual is almost sovereign; if two adults consent together to have sexual relations what business is it of anyone else? As far as the Bible is concerned, no man is an island. Everyone inhabits a context: family, community, society. I am my brother's keeper and what I do affects other people. How I behave affects my parents and my children; it affects my relations and my neighbours; it promotes community or divides it. Secondly, the attention given to prohibiting incestuous relationships means that these passages are concerned with sexual behaviour rather than simply with pagan fertility rites.

In Leviticus 18 the prohibition on male homosexual intercourse comes at the end of the list of prohibited relationships between the prohibition of child sacrifice and bestiality. Quite clearly these are grouped together as particularly serious. In Leviticus 20 the grouping is somewhat different. There is a group of sexual relationships that require the death penalty first, and this is followed by a further list with lesser penalties. That male homosexual intercourse is in the first grouping requiring the death penalty again indicates its seriousness. In both passages homosexual intercourse is described as 'an abomination'. While idolatry is also similarly described, the way the word is used here indicates that it is the seriousness of this sin, rather than any connection with idolatry, that is being underscored. In Leviticus 18:21, to offer a child to Molech is to 'profane the name of God'. In verse 23 bestiality is 'a perversion'. In each case the gravity of the sin is emphasised.

It is sometimes argued that as the death penalty appears to be abrogated by the New Testament it cannot be argued that the prohibition of homosexual intercourse continues in force. But this does not follow. It cannot seriously be argued that the prohibition of adultery, or child sacrifice, or bestiality has been abrogated along with the death penalty for those sins and there are no objective grounds for simply exempting homosexual behaviour.

Determining on what grounds the death penalty is to be thought of as no longer applicable in cases to which it applied in the Old Testament requires an understanding of how the two Testaments are related together. Indeed, the whole question of how we understand the relevance of the law given by Moses to the era introduced by the coming of Christ is also of great importance. But neither of these matters is decisive for our present purpose because the New Testament, as we shall see, also includes homosexual intercourse among other behaviours that exclude from the kingdom of God. What is prohibited in Leviticus is also prohibited in Romans, 1 Corinthians and 1 Timothy. There is therefore a consistency about the biblical witness.

Moreover, how exactly to understand the death penalty in the Mosaic law is not straightforward. In Matthew 15 we read of Jesus speaking to the Pharisees and scribes: 'And why do you break the commandment of God for the sake of your tradition? For God commanded, "Honour your father and your mother" and, "Whoever reviles father or mother must surely die." But you say, "If anyone tells his father or mother, What you would have gained from me is given to God, he need not honour his father." So for the sake of your tradition you have made void the word of God.' Here we have a close parallel to what we have seen in Leviticus. Jesus first quotes the commandment; then he quotes the commandment plus penalty from the next chapter. And his words are strong; the Authorized Version is not far off the original with its 'let him die the death'.

This does not necessarily mean that we ought to think the penalty still applies in the way it did when it was given. In Jesus' day the Jews did not have authority to carry out the death penalty nor was there any danger of the Jews doing that in this case, even if it was within their power. Why did Jesus refer to the penalty? The most likely explanation is that he was reminding the Pharisees that God would judge them one day and he would consider their behaviour a very serious matter. If we take the view that the death penalty for sins like this is no longer to be applied since Jesus came and a new trans-national entity, the church, has come into being, that does not mean we can forget all about penalty; there will be a penalty to pay one day for those whose sins are not forgiven. Jesus spoke as he did because the Pharisees had devised a way of getting round the fifth commandment and this is a reminder to those Christians who try to argue that the prohibition of homosexuality in Leviticus is irrelevant that they had better make sure their arguments are absolutely watertight.

These verses in Leviticus lay the emphasis on what is not to be *done*: 'You shall not lie with a male as with a woman.' This is an emphasis found in all the references we shall be looking at in the Bible; it is behaviour that is prohibited. Motive and psychology are not mentioned (though this does not mean that the Bible does not enable us to give attention to these). Men are men and so they are not to relate sexually to other men. Orientation is important in our day and something has been said about that in the previous chapter, but the Bible focuses on actions in this matter.

These laws were given by God through Moses and written down by him. But it was Moses who also wrote Genesis with the Sodom narrative in chapter 19. There is a complete consistency between the laws of Leviticus and the tone and content of Genesis 19. As we noticed, Sodom was ripe for judgement much earlier than the rest of Canaan, but the same sins were found in Sodom as among the Canaanite tribes, and these were prohibited to the Israelites. Among these was homosexual behaviour.

There is one more passage in the Old Testament that deserves a brief mention. It comes in Judges 19 and concerns a Levite who took a concubine from Bethlehem. The relevant part of the story takes place in Gibeah of Benjamin, where the Levite and his concubine sought refuge for the night. An old man on his return from the fields took them into his house:

As they were making their hearts merry, behold, the men of the city, worthless fellows, surrounded the house, beating on the door. And they said to the old man, the master of the house, 'Bring out the man who came into your house, that we may know him.' And the man, the master of the house, went out to them, and said to them, 'No, my brothers, do not act so wickedly; since this man has come into my house, do not do this vile thing. Behold, here are my virgin daughter and his concubine. Let me bring them out now. Violate them and do with them what seems good to you, but against this man do not do this outrageous thing.'   Judges 19:22–24

In the event only the concubine was given to them and she was abused all night and taken up dead in the morning.

This appalling incident in many ways mirrors what took place at Sodom. It does not add to what we have already seen, but three comments can be made. Firstly, this confirms what we saw in the case of Sodom that homosexual violation was looked upon as worse than heterosexual violation. This lies on the face of the narrative. Secondly, there can be no question of hospitality codes being involved here; the old man offered not only his daughter but also the Levite's concubine. Thirdly, this, of course, took place in Israel. Here 'in those days, when there was no king in Israel' (19:1), was a city that had declined so much from the ways of the Lord and had followed the ways of the Canaanites so much, that it was in a fair way to becoming a second Sodom. Centuries later what happened at Gibeah was not forgotten: 'They have deeply corrupted themselves as in the days of Gibeah' (Hosea 9:9; see also 10:9).

Romans 1:18–32

For the wrath of God is revealed from heaven against all ungodliness and unrighteousness of men, who by their unrighteousness suppress the truth. For what can be known about God is plain to them, because God has shown it to them. For his invisible attributes, namely, his eternal power and divine nature, have been clearly perceived, ever since the creation of the world, in the things that have been made. So they are without excuse. For although they knew God, they did not honour him as God or give thanks to him, but they became futile in their thinking, and their foolish hearts were darkened. Claiming to be wise, they became fools, and exchanged the glory of the immortal God for images resembling mortal man and birds and animals and reptiles.

Therefore God gave them up in the lusts of their hearts to impurity, to the dishonouring of their bodies among themselves, because they exchanged the truth about God for a lie and worshipped and served the creature rather than the Creator, who is blessed forever! Amen.

For this reason God gave them up to dishonourable passions. For their women exchanged natural relations for those that are contrary to nature; and the men likewise gave up natural relations with women and were consumed with passion for one another, men committing shameless acts with men and receiving in themselves the due penalty for their error.

And since they did not see fit to acknowledge God, God gave them up to a debased mind to do what ought not to be done. They were filled with all manner of unrighteousness, evil, covetousness, malice. They are full of envy, murder, strife, deceit, maliciousness. They are gossips, slanderers, haters of God, insolent, haughty, boastful, inventors of evil, disobedient to parents, foolish, faithless, heartless, ruthless. Though they know God's decree that those who practise such things deserve to die, they not only do them but give approval to those who practise them.

This is the first passage in the New Testament to refer to homosexual practice and the whole section is given in order to show the context and the connection between the verses. Some general comments are in order first of all. In this passage Paul is demonstrating that God's wrath is revealed from heaven against human ungodliness and unrighteousness. This is seen in the way in which God gives people up to evils which are already present within them. In the first place this is to 'the lusts of their hearts to impurity' which expresses itself in 'the dishonouring of their bodies among themselves'. Secondly, it is to 'dishonourable passions' and thirdly to 'a debased mind to do what ought not to be done' which results in people's lives being filled with 'all manner of unrighteousness', which is spelled out in some detail though of course not exhaustively.

There does not appear to be a particular order here as if there were any intensifying of God's wrath, God giving up people more and more as they got worse and worse. The final list of evils seems to rule this out; rather what we have here are different examples of the way God gives people and societies up. In verses 24 and 25 there may be a particular connection with what is said in verse 23. Because people degrade God by making him in the image of themselves or animals and such like, so God gives people up to degrade themselves. Made in the image of God they abuse their bodies and deface the dignity with which God endowed them. It may be this is to be understood of sexual behaviour—certainly it would seem to include it— but it may equally refer to violence. People become worse than wild animals in their cruelty towards each other with their bloodshed and wars.

The crucial verses are 26 and 27 in which homosexual practices are described as resulting from dishonourable passions. It is the homosexual behaviour of women and men which demonstrates the dishonourable passions from which it springs; this is the sense of the 'for'—'for their women exchanged natural relations for those that are contrary to nature'. This is the only place in the Bible where lesbianism is explicitly mentioned. It is possible that the prohibition of male-with-male sex was understood as implying a corresponding prohibition of female-to-female relations. It may also be that lesbianism was not nearly so common, or possibly it was considered as virtually unmentionable (cf. Ephesians 5:12). However, this one place shows that according to Paul the natural sexual relations for women are with men and so women-to-women relations are contrary to nature. To express it like this is actually stronger than a simple prohibition; such relations are not what ought to be.

This verse and the next speak about what is 'natural'. On the surface the meaning of this seems quite obvious, but there has been debate about it because it is said that Paul can use the word to refer to what is customary (e.g. 1 Corinthians 11:14–15) or to the way people are (e.g. Romans 2:14). It is then argued that because some people are homosexual by nature—that is the way they are—therefore what Paul says here cannot apply to them. However, whatever may be the case with other references we have to see what 'natural' means in its present context.

We can note first that the context is one in which Paul is speaking about creation and the Creator (especially vv.20,25). In this context what is natural must be understood in terms of the Creator's purpose and not in terms of what people may feel is natural to them. If God gives people up to dishonourable passions then it is not surprising if they want to express these. To then argue that because these are 'natural' for those people such people do not come under the rest of verses 26–27 is a most extraordinary and perverse type of logic.

But it is also surely clear that Paul is simply appealing to what is obvious by considering the anatomical differentiation between male and female and the function of intercourse in reproduction. Petersen, perhaps in context referring to the work of Gagnon, says, 'For Paul it was a simple matter of observation that homosexual intercourse was "contrary to nature", so that pagans who were ignorant of the biblical record had no excuse for not knowing God's purpose for the sexual organs.'[5]

In verse 27 Paul goes on to consider the case of males and he has more to say. Firstly, he says, the men gave up 'natural relations with women'. This phrase in itself indicates what he means by 'natural'. He then goes on to speak of them being 'consumed with passion for one another'. 'Consumed' is a strong word, literally meaning 'burning', while 'passion' is a different word from that used in verse 26 and means something like 'eagerness'— 'burning with eagerness for one another'. In considering this we must remember that Paul is talking in a general way of societies that 'worship and serve the creature rather than the Creator' (v.25). He is not picking on particular individuals; though of course there will be individuals of whom this is true. And although he is talking of homosexual desire here this is but the unnatural expression of improper and unfettered sexual desire, it is a particular way of 'dishonouring ... their bodies among themselves' (v.24). Similarly in Ephesians 4:19 he speaks of Gentiles who 'have given themselves up to sensuality', and 'are greedy to practise every kind of impurity'.

The next clause speaks of 'men with men committing shameless acts', or 'what is shameless' (or 'shameful' depending on how you look at it). Here Paul tells us that the acts that homosexual men take part in between themselves are shameful. Nothing could be plainer than this. These are acts that ought not to be committed; they constitute an abuse of sexuality and the sexual organs. However we understand the origin of orientation, and however much sympathy we may have for people who only feel sexually attracted to those of the same sex, the acts themselves are wrong.

In the final clause Paul says, 'and receiving in themselves the due penalty for their error'. While 'due penalty' is an acceptable translation, more literally it is 'the recompense they ought to (receive)'. Leon Morris says of this, 'Paul is not so much calling for a penalty as thinking of sexual perversion as itself a penalty (being a sinner is the punishment of sin!).'[6] This seems to understand 'their error' as referring to worshipping and serving the creature rather than the Creator (v.25), rather than the dishonourable passions and their outcome in homosexual behaviour (v.26). On the surface it looks more likely to be the latter, but we cannot be sure precisely which he is speaking about. It may be possible to combine the two ideas in that burning with sexual desire can become a self-perpetuating thing; the more you express it the more you want to do so again.

Two final comments can be made. The beginning of chapter 2 of this letter reads like this: 'Therefore you have no excuse, O man, every one of you who judges. For in passing judgment on another you condemn yourself, because you, the judge, practise the very same things.' It is very likely that Paul is here turning to the Jews who had a strong tendency to condemn the Gentiles for their immoral behaviour. The point cannot be that those who condemned others committed exactly the same outward sins to the same degree; Paul obviously has in mind 'sanctimonious persons' (Calvin) whose lifestyle appeared superior and who consequently felt in a position to judge and condemn.[7] It is a warning we all need, for it is all too easy to adopt a judgemental, condemnatory spirit.

Secondly, while it is true that the verses we have been considering come in the context of the wrath of God (v.18), that itself comes in as the background from which Paul glories in the gospel and is eager to preach it (v.15): 'For I am not ashamed of the gospel, for it is the power of God for salvation to everyone who believes' (v.16). Paul's concern at the end of chapter 1 is to highlight the need for the gospel and to prepare the way for the explanation of that gospel which comes in 3:21 to the end of chapter 5. Paul's main interest is to set out the forgiving, justifying grace of God through our Lord Jesus Christ. That must never be forgotten.

1 Corinthians 6:9–11

Do you not know that the unrighteous will not inherit the kingdom of God? Do not be deceived: neither the sexually immoral, nor idolaters, nor adulterers, nor men who practise homosexuality, nor thieves, nor the greedy, nor drunkards, nor revilers, nor swindlers will inherit the kingdom of God. And such were some of you. But you were washed, you were sanctified, you were justified in the name of the Lord Jesus Christ and by the Spirit of our God.

The operative words are 'nor men who practise homosexuality'. This may be correct so far as it goes, but there are actually two words that are used here. It is sometimes argued that there is uncertainty about what they mean, and therefore we cannot be certain about Paul's precise intention here. But the strong likelihood is that the words refer to the active and passive partners in homosexual intercourse. This is discernible rather than explicit in the standard lexicon of Walter Bauer[8] while the Louw and Nida lexicon says of the first word, 'the passive male partner in homosexual intercourse', and of the second, 'It is possible ... in certain contexts [it] refers to the active male partner...' It also comments: 'As in Greek, a number of other languages also have entirely distinct terms for the active and passive roles in homosexual intercourse.'[9] Even if there is a small element of doubt about the usage of the two terms, there is no doubt that it is those who practise homosexuality who are being referred to.

Once more the context is important. It is a clear warning: 'Do not be deceived'; people who consistently behave in these ways 'will not inherit the kingdom of God.' Nor is it out of place to draw attention to what Paul goes on to say from verse 12, where he warns against sexual immorality. It is true he is speaking about heterosexual immorality, but his words are striking:

The body is not meant for sexual immorality, but for the Lord, and the Lord for the body ... Flee from sexual immorality. Every other sin a person commits is outside the body, but the sexually immoral person sins against his own body. Or do you not know that your body is a temple of the Holy Spirit within you, whom you have from God? (vv.13,18–19)

These words indicate that not only does sexual sin damage marriage and family life but it is an abuse of the body God has given us. We sin against our own bodies, given to us by God in which to serve and glorify him and, for Christians, indwelt by the Holy Spirit for this purpose. However, we must also never forget the encouraging words of verse 11: 'And such were some of you. But you were washed, you were sanctified, you were justified in the name of the Lord Jesus Christ and by the Spirit of our God.'

1 Timothy 1:8–12

Now we know that the law is good, if one uses it lawfully, understanding this, that the law is not laid down for the just but for the lawless and disobedient, for the ungodly and sinners, for the unholy and profane, for those who strike their fathers and mothers, for murderers, the sexually immoral, men who practise homosexuality, enslavers, liars, perjurers, and whatever else is contrary to sound doctrine, in accordance with the glorious gospel of the blessed God with which I have been entrusted.

The first thing to note is that the word translated here 'men who practise homosexuality' is actually the second word used by Paul in the previous passage; more literally it is 'those who lie with men'. Secondly, and more importantly, what does Paul mean by 'law' in this place? The verse before this passage refers to those who desire 'to be teachers of the law'. G.W. Knight points out that in the only other two places where the same word (literally it is 'law-teachers') is used in the New Testament it clearly means 'teachers of the Mosaic law', and he gives additional reasons for understanding it in that way here.[10] The particular sins listed all seem to reflect the ten commandments, and the most serious breaches of those commandments. Not merely those who dishonour father and mother, but those who 'strike their fathers and mothers'; not merely those who steal, but those who kidnap people to sell into slavery. This makes it likely that the sins of 'the sexually immoral' and 'men who practise homosexuality' are both considered breaches of the commandment: 'You shall not commit adultery.' It is not at all impossible that Paul would consider the verses in Leviticus 18 and 20 that we have already examined as an application of that commandment. At any rate he sees a continuing relevance in the law and looks upon it as given particularly 'for the lawless and disobedient', perhaps both to restrain sin and also to convince those who break it that they are sinning against God and therefore in need of forgiveness. Timothy was in Ephesus (v. 3), so Paul understands the law as functioning beyond the nation of Israel.

As Jude 7 was considered earlier, that completes our survey of the references to homosexual practice in the Bible. When we think of the size of the Bible these references are very few, but it is important not to think of the books of the Bible as a collection of varied autonomous texts. If we think of the Bible as existing first in the mind of God and then written by different men at different times under the guidance of the Holy Spirit we realise there is a fundamental unity. We can look at this in a slightly different way also. As the books of the Old Testament were produced they functioned as the theological and devotional literature of Israel, moulding the thinking and conduct of the people. So the later writers were nurtured in the earlier writings. And the same is true of the New Testament. Its writers show their knowledge and dependence on the Old Testament. So there is a consistency about the whole Bible.

Some of those who argue for a Christian acceptance of homosexual practice maintain that what the Bible has to say needs to be understood as having only a limited reference. There are two ways in which this is argued. Firstly, it is said that we know now that some people have a homosexual orientation, but as this was not known in biblical times the Bible cannot be directly speaking about people in such a position. But this is an argument from silence, which is always dangerous. It is difficult to believe that Paul, with his profound understanding of the power of sin in the inward heart, would not trace the origin of homosexual desire to the heart. Indeed, is that not precisely what he does in Romans 1 when he speaks of 'men … consumed with passion for one another'? The whole subject is not easy as the previous chapter has acknowledged. In any case, in these passages we have been considering the emphasis on activity. Whatever the causes it is homosexual activity which the Bible prohibits.

The second way in which it is sometimes maintained that these passages are irrelevant is by saying that they are not referring to the loving relationships that some Christians argue are permissible. Rather, these passages have in view heterosexuals whose promiscuity crosses the boundary into same-sex relationships. They are not looking for committed relationships; they are looking for sexual pleasure in whatever way they can get it. That the Bible certainly prohibits such depraved behaviour is obvious and we have already commented on the way this was true of the men of Sodom. But the fact is that the Bible knows nothing of the loving same-sex relationships that are argued for and it does prohibit the sexual activity that would take place within them.

This chapter is inevitably negative in tone. But the Bible in its overall thrust is not negative. To follow the wrong way is never best even if that way sometimes seems right to us (see Proverbs 14:12). To fear the Lord and follow the way of wisdom is always best, for 'her ways are ways of pleasantness, and all her paths are peace' (Proverbs 3:17).

Notes

1 **Kevin J. Vanhoozer,** *The Drama of Doctrine* (Westminster: John Knox Press, 2005), p. 70. Author's italics.

2 **David Petersen** in **Petersen, ed.,** *Holiness and Sexuality* (Carlisle: Paternoster, 2004), p. 3.

3 **Gordon J. Wenham,** 'Genesis 16–50', *Word Biblical Commentary* (Waco: Word Books, 1994), p. 63.

4 **G. Ch. Alders,** *Genesis,* Vol. 2 (Grand Rapids: Zondervan, 1981), p. 16.

5 *Op. cit.*, p. 46.

6 **Leon Morris,** *The Epistle to the Romans* (Leicester: IVP, 1988), p. 93.

7 These sentences come from 'Exegesis 4: Romans 1, Homosexuality and Aids', which I contributed to *Foundations*: no. 18; spring 1987, p. 6.

8 **Walter Bauer,** *A Greek-English Lexicon of the New Testament and Other Early Christian Literature*, second edition, revised and augmented by **Wilbur Gingrich** and **Frederick W. Danker** (University of Chicago Press, 1979), pp. 488, 109.

9 **Johannes P. Louw** and **Eugene A. Nida,** *Greek-English Lexicon of the New Testament based on Semantic Domains*, second edition (United Bible Societies, 1989), vol. 1, p. 772.

10 **George W. Knight III,** *The Pastoral Epistles,* The New Testament Greek Commentary (Grand Rapids: Eerdmans and Carlisle: Paternoster Press, 1992), p. 79.

Equality for whom?

Roger Hitchings

Discrimination has been an area of great debate as homosexual activists have sought to redress the oppression and injustices they perceive that they have encountered through many centuries. However, the focus of discrimination appears to be changing. Many of the concerns of the homosexual community have been addressed by numerous changes to the law and public perception. And while there still may be some ingrained discrimination against them in some sectors of society, it is increasingly evangelical Christians who now find themselves facing discrimination.

'Prejudice, ignorance, apathy and fear lead to discrimination. Discrimination denies our human dignity, our freedom to be ourselves, and our place in a free society. When even one person is deprived of one of these basic human rights, we are all diminished.'[1]

Christians are concerned about justice. They are opposed to prejudice and discrimination which leads to people being denied the dignity and respect that is their due as human beings. Christians have fought tirelessly to redress disadvantage and to bring relief to the oppressed. The history of the Christian church overflows with wonderful examples of women and men who have identified with the poor and those who suffer, and who have worked tirelessly to redress injustice and cruelty. The Bible clearly teaches the importance of doing good to those in need as an evidence of a true faith in Christ (see, for example, Psalm 82:3–4; Galatians 2:10; James 1:27), and the Christian church, when she has been faithful to the truth of the gospel, has always sought to be the defender of 'the orphan and the widow'. So evangelical Christians have been at the forefront of many of the social advances which have improved the lot of women, men and children throughout the world. Indeed, there is impressive evidence that this continues to be the case in our world today. Christians have always been at the forefront of those who have fought against intolerance and have advocated that people should be respected because of who they are, even when what they believe or teach is contrary to the beliefs that we hold dear.

True Christians have always sought to implement the teachings of Jesus, and have taken seriously the words he spoke in the Beatitudes in Matthew 5: 'Blessed are the merciful,' 'Blessed are the peacemakers.' So where there have been injustice and cruelty they have sought to introduce mercy and compassion. Where there have been aggression and troubled hearts they have endeavoured to bring peace both through the message of Christ and by practical involvement in meeting the needs of people around them. The whole concept of tolerance has been at the centre of Christian thinking. They have been directed by the principle that people are to be respected as 'made in the image of God' and so treated with compassion, although their ideas and practice are against the law of God.

We live in a fast-changing society, however, where accepted attitudes and perspectives are challenged in most unexpected ways. Nowhere is this clearer than in the area of tolerance. In a society that respects individual freedoms, tolerance is seen in an openness to others and acceptance of them as people, although their ideas and lifestyles may be challenged. As Don Carson expresses it, 'This robust toleration for people, if not always for their ideas, engenders a measure of civility in public discourse while still fostering spirited debate over the relative merits of this or that idea.'[2] This understanding of tolerance has been a part of the warp and woof of western society. Christians must testify to God's truth and warn people of the dangers of their sins, for the message we preach reminds everyone that we are ultimately accountable to him and he will judge everyone himself. But at the same time we respect and love men and women who have different views from us because they are 'in God's image'. For Bible-believing Christians, tolerance is strengthened by our understanding and acceptance of God's justice.

Justice, as the Bible teaches it, not only requires fair dealing for everyone in society, but also the promotion of righteousness and the rejection of sin and sinful behaviour (for example, Micah 6:8; Isaiah 1:16–17; Zechariah 7:9–10). That means that some lifestyles must be challenged because they are contrary to the truth and law of God. Those who practise these lifestyles must be loved, but their values and behaviour must be opposed and rejected. Such a stance will be misunderstood by those who have chosen that lifestyle, and also by those who are unprepared to accept the authority of God as expressed in the Bible. It can also be misunderstood by Christians who with a false zeal fail to show Christlike love and compassion to those whose lifestyles they feel duty-bound to oppose. In all honesty, Christians have to admit that in the past, and even at present, there have been wrong attitudes towards those who have chosen a homosexual lifestyle. In opposing that which is sinful, some Christians have at times also fallen into the trap of behaving with unjustifiable intolerance and even cruelty. The claim by homosexual activists that for centuries they have been robbed of their essential human dignity has some justification.

So Christians, in faithfulness to the teachings of the Bible, seek to promote a society where there is tolerance of people, but a rejection of things that are harmful to others and wrong in the sight of God. Such a view of toleration has been in the mainstream of western thought for generations. But as we have already noted, the world has changed. Tolerance in western thinking has increasingly focused on ideas and not on people. To some degree this is partly due to the view of pluralism that now dominates. For some people the concept of pluralism simply means that society has become increasingly diverse and this has to be accepted without prejudice. But in reality the whole concept of what is true and whether anyone has 'truth' is now discounted. Ideas are to be tolerated because no one is right and no one is wrong. This has changed the way society deals with issues. Again, quoting Don Carson:

The result of adopting this new brand of tolerance is less discussion of the merits of competing ideas—and less civility. There is less discussion because toleration of diverse ideas demands that we avoid criticising the opinions of others … There is less civility because there is no inherent demand, in this new practice of tolerance, to be tolerant of people, and it is especially difficult to be tolerant of those people whose views are so far outside the accepted 'plausibility structures' that they think your brand of tolerance is muddleheaded.[3]

It is fair to say that increasingly this is how biblical Christianity is viewed, especially by those within the homosexual community.

A growing intolerance

Those who advocate a homosexual lifestyle have demanded acceptance within society and the removal of all prejudice. This chapter will show how this has been, and is being, achieved through legislation and public practice. What they appear unable, or unwilling, to accept or allow is that there are those who have a legitimate alternative view. In fact their claims are couched in terms that require, for instance, that evangelical Christians must deny what they believe and must sacrifice their commitment to the Bible as the sole authority for life. It seems that the issues of prejudice are beginning to change, and that with more and more acceptance being given to homosexual perspectives and values it is those who oppose who become the disadvantaged. Tolerance has been extended to a great extent to homosexuals, but they seem increasingly to demand that it be withdrawn from those who disagree with them.

A glaring example of these excessive demands and intolerant responses to those who oppose them was seen in two conflicting articles in *The London Times* on Saturday 23 October 2004 and Monday 25 October 2004. The first article was by Matthew Parris. Mr Parris writes regular columns in *The Times* and *The Spectator*. On moral issues he regularly writes from a homosexual perspective. The second article was by William Rees-Mogg, and was written to answer Matthew Parris's article. William Rees-Mogg is a writer and scholar, and a regular commentator in *The Times*; he served as its editor from 1961 to 1981.

The cause of the debate was events that had taken place in the European Parliament during the previous week. The Parliament had been holding hearings to examine proposed European Commissioners. Rocco Buttiglione, the nominated Italian Commissioner, had been proposed as Commissioner for Justice. He was asked whether his adherence to the Roman Catholic teaching that homosexuality is a sin would interfere with his work as the Commissioner responsible for civil liberties. The question was a trap. He replied that he did indeed regard homosexuality as a sin, but not as a crime; he quoted Kant's distinction between morality and law as justification for his position. Following this reply there was an outcry that he was a homophobe who should not be allowed to have the job.

Matthew Parris, described by William Rees-Mogg as 'normally an apostle of toleration', expressed very strong views about such religiously-based thinking: 'I say: enough of tolerance. I do not tolerate religious superstition, not when it refuses to tolerate me. Sweep it from the corridors of power.'4 He then went on to defend this view:

There are Christians and Christians, as there are Muslims and Muslims, Jews and Jews and Hindus and Hindus. But well within the mainstreams of all four faiths are to be found core beliefs which now lie right outside the mainstream of modern European thought. Let me mention a few. Catholic, evangelical Christian, Orthodox, Judaic and Muslim teaching on homosexuality and divorce; much Muslim practice as to the status of women; some Hindu teaching on caste; and Catholic teaching on contraception and abortion are insulting, not only to me but also to the majority of Europeans, and the overwhelming majority of educated Europeans. I do not shrink from according special status to the educated, for they lead thought.

This extraordinary idea that 'educated Europeans' have a higher moral understanding than simple folk is very elitist and arrogant. But it will be seen how the paramount issue is one of ideas. To this way of thinking any rejection of homosexuality as an acceptable lifestyle must be regarded as a total rejection of the person as well. The civility that once would have been seen in discussion, and the faithful representation of an opposite viewpoint that goes with that civility, are ominously absent. A whole plethora of long-established religious and moral perspectives are swept away because they are out of line with the thinking of 'the overwhelming majority of educated Europeans'. There is no discussion of the value of these ideas or their intrinsic worth. They disagree with a stated point of view and so they are not to be accorded tolerance.

Rees-Mogg's reply takes a very broad stance that expresses considerable toleration of private sexual relationships: 'It is no business of the State to impose its own or any Church's view of religious doctrine on its citizens. This extends to some broad questions of morality. In general, the State should stay out of the bedroom, though it cannot do so completely. There will always be police issues in sexual assault and rape.' He then proceeds to examine Catholic teaching on homosexuality with fairness and sympathy, something Parris did not do. Having done so he concludes his analysis by correctly pointing out that

There is, of course, a wide difference between Catholic sexual teaching and what Matthew calls modern European thought. Modern European thought is post-Freudian and utilitarian. It places a very high value on self-expression but a lower value on stability and fidelity. Promiscuity is accepted, and sometimes regarded with enthusiasm. Sex of all types is likely to be regarded as a good in itself. In short, modern European thought concentrates on the hedonistic benefit of the individual.

This is a powerful critique of the difference between a 'Christian' viewpoint (and in the main the Catholic Church does reflect a biblical understanding on this issue) and the developing approach to tolerance. Rees-Mogg's conclusion is very significant: 'Matthew wants to pull up the anchors of Judaism, Catholicism, Protestantism, Islam and Hinduism. With them he would avowedly also pull up the anchor of tolerance.'

That is, of course, the serious issue for Bible-believing Christians. A key aspect of the view expressed by Matthew Parris is this idea that 'I do not tolerate religious superstition, not when it refuses to tolerate me.' Evangelical Christianity is to him a religious superstition. As an atheist and a homosexual he is a brilliant spokesman for many within the homosexual community. He presents a caricature of Christian tolerance in which the denial of the acceptability of a homosexual lifestyle is a denial of every homosexual. His views dramatically illustrate the situation in which we now find ourselves. Tolerance is about ideas. To call something wrong is unacceptable. It is a rejection of the person. In this world of thought, evangelical Christians are the unacceptable ones and should not be tolerated. It is undoubtedly the case that this rejection of a biblical perspective is found across society.

A rethink on rights

In the public arena, therefore, evangelical Christians increasingly find themselves holding minority views that strongly conflict with the general tenor and drift of public opinion. This is not a new position for Christians. The believers in the first centuries of the church faced this dilemma constantly, and at times joyfully paid a heavy price. What is new for us is that there is also an increasingly adverse legal framework in which Christians have to live and work.

The homosexual lobby has vociferously demanded its 'rights'. What those 'rights' are have been defined by themselves rather than by any external authority or standard. They have argued, lobbied, publicly demonstrated and, it has to acknowledged, even intimidated until they have achieved their goals. Their claim has been 'gay rights equal human rights', and the comprehensive list of goals they have pursued has shown their intolerance of all other perspectives. The Christian Institute, an evangelical lobby group, has rightly responded by pointing out that human rights in respect of lifestyle should only refer to religion or issues of physical or generic characteristics, e.g. disability and race. So they point out that 'sexual practice is a moral choice. It is not a religion. Nor is it a physical or generic characteristic. It is a choice.'[5] They argue that studies show that social factors, rather than genetics, lead to most homosexual practice.

But this argument is now being dismissed by homosexual activists, and by those involved in forming public opinion. In an article entitled 'Nature? Nurture? It Doesn't Matter', John Corvino argues as follows:

One of the most persistent debates surrounding homosexuality regards whether gays are 'born that way' or whether homosexuality is a 'chosen lifestyle'. The debate is ill-formed from the start, in that it conflates two separate questions: How did you become what you are? (By genetics? Early environment? Wilful choice? Some combination of the above?), and Can you change what you are?

Moreover, the fact that feelings are strong doesn't mean that they're genetically determined. They might be, but they might not. Sexual orientation's involuntariness, which is largely beyond dispute, is separate from its origin, which is still controversial, even among sympathetic scientists.

... we do not determine whether a trait is good by looking at where it came from (genetics, environment, or something else). We determine whether it is good by looking at its effects.

Nor does it matter whether sexual orientation can be changed. For even if it could (which is doubtful in most cases), it doesn't follow that it should.[6]

He then quotes a speech from 1964:

In a 1964 speech to the New York Mattachine Society, an early gay rights group, activist Frank Kameny announced: 'We are interested in obtaining rights for our respective minorities as Negroes, as Jews, and as Homosexuals. Why we are Negroes, Jews, or Homosexuals is totally irrelevant, and whether we can be changed to Whites, Christians or heterosexuals is equally irrelevant.'

There are clearly assumptions in what he says that evangelical Christians would wish to challenge. But the main point he makes, and which reflects a growing argument, is that the origin or cause of homosexuality is irrelevant. What matters is the present choice of each individual. This rejection of the argument that nature or nurture is important is becoming generally accepted within society. In a lecture at King's College, London reported by CARE on its website,[7] Dame Elizabeth Butler-Sloss, probably the leading family law judge, argued for extending full legal rights to homosexual partnerships and for the permitting of transsexuals to marry in their self-selected gender. She claimed that to fail to do so was to 'fail the family'. The issue of selecting a lifestyle was seen as equivalent and equally valid to being born with an orientation to that lifestyle.

This brings us back to the discussion between Matthew Parris and William Rees-Mogg and the prevailing 'modern European thought' which is 'post-Freudian and utilitarian'. It is now the contention of both popular opinion, and also the legal framework, as it affects employment and public discourse, that homosexuality is as valid as heterosexuality as a lifestyle. The fact that it may be a chosen aspect of life rather than a religion or a physical or generic characteristic is no longer considered relevant. That is reflected most powerfully in the entertainment world and most of the media. And this position increasingly threatens to leave evangelical Christians as a disadvantaged minority.

A need for wisdom

The homosexual lobby is not satisfied with the progress it has made so far. The law has changed dramatically in favour of homosexuals in many areas, but they want yet more. Some of the future issues will be considered below.

In this changing and very confused climate Christians must seek to be both compassionate towards all men and women, and also faithful to the inviolable truth they have in the Bible. We must seek to display justice and love as our Saviour did. The classic example for us is his conduct in John 7:53–8:11. There he showed both love and understanding to a disadvantaged and misused woman while also upholding the high moral values of God's law. And he did that against the tide of popular opinion and public sentiment. Don Carson puts the Christian responsibility in this way, 'Christians must constantly articulate *and display* the nature of true tolerance. Whilst we insist that objective truth exists, that the personal/transcendent God can be known, that religious claims in conflict with Christ are necessarily false, we must also publicly and repeatedly disavow coerced belief and insist on the right of others to disagree with us.'[8] So we must continue to declare that a homosexual lifestyle is wrong and sinful, yet at the same time we must show the fullest respect and love to those who practise these unacceptable lifestyles. This is the old tolerance, but the one that reflects biblical teaching.

Changing legislation and new concerns

There have been vast changes in the legal status of those who follow a homosexual lifestyle. Before looking at the issues that will challenge Christians, it is important to consider some of the most recent changes and how they will affect the lives of many Christians.

STATUTORY PROTECTION OF THE VULNERABLE

Parliament repealed Section 28 of the Local Government Act (1988) in July 2003. This piece of legislation prevented local authorities from spending money on the promotion of homosexuality in schools or elsewhere and from promoting a homosexual lifestyle as a 'pretended family relationship'. Since that decision there have been a few instances of local authorities and health authorities producing materials that would have fallen foul of the legislation. The chief impact, however, appears to be a more provocative and daring approach to sex education in general which many Christians would find offensive. Parents' groups in areas such as Glasgow have held strong protests. Aids awareness programmes run by health authorities are also now more open in promoting homosexuality as an acceptable lifestyle. The Christian Institute,[9] whose lobbying and informative work on all these matters is second to none and deserves the maximum support, has carefully monitored these developments.

This is an area where Christians will increasingly feel beleaguered and discriminated against. There are actions that may be taken. Christian parents need to be fully aware of the materials being used in their children's schools, and be prepared to challenge the things they find unacceptable. A particular illustration of this was cited in the *Daily Mail* on 4 November 2005: 'The Qualifications and Curriculum Authority (QCA) says primary schools need to cover a wider range of relationships than the traditional nuclear family of a mother, father and 2.4 children. This could include same-sex families, single parents and children who are looked after in local authority care.' Groups of Christians may seek to prepare alternative materials that are less offensive. Individual parents have the right to withdraw their children from lessons that use unacceptable materials or practices. Similarly churches and individual Christians need to be ready to question the materials and presentations made by health authorities. It cannot be stressed enough how important it is to know what is going on and to be ready to speak out with grace and wisdom, but also with forcefulness and cogency. Silence by individual Christians and churches on these matters in their local areas is not an option if we are to be 'salt and light' in our communities.

Another area of change has been the age of consent for homosexual sex. This was lowered to sixteen in January 2001, and the age at which girls could be subjected to buggery was also lowered to sixteen. This gave the clear message that homosexual and heterosexual activities are morally equivalent. It also means that while children are protected from sexual abuse under Child Protection measures until they are eighteen, the reality of seduction by a homosexual man, for instance, of a seventeen-year-old boy is no longer a crime. It needs to be remembered that legalising homosexual acts with teenage boys puts them at risk because they are at an age when they can be vulnerable to sexual approaches from other males, especially older men. Teenage boys can be very confused about their sexual attractions.

There are those in the homosexual community who would wish to see the age of consent further reduced, and this is a further matter that all Christians must carefully monitor. This removal of protection from young people will produce a harvest of sorrow in the future lives of many. Christians again need to face up to this challenge by doing all they can to teach biblical standards of morality, and to provide a compassionate and supportive environment for those who are put under unfair pressures, or who are hurt by activities they become involved with. Parents need to be alert to some of the materials publicly displayed in schools, and ready to protest. Pastors and church leaders, in particular, must be alert to the needs of young people within their own congregations and those who may be attending youth activities. The need for wholesome and positive outlets for young people becomes even more highlighted by this issue.

A further major change that has already presented problems to Christians is the approval of homosexual couples to adopt. The experience of social workers in Sefton as documented by the Christian Institute[10] demonstrates the problems that may well arise in the future. An attempt to insert an opt-out clause for social workers who oppose unmarried adoption was rejected by the Government. The issue of freedom of conscience for those who work in the public services will be an increasingly vexed matter in the years to come. Once more pastors and church leaders must keep themselves informed of what is happening in general within our society, and especially of what is happening with those in their congregations who face these difficult situations.

These three issues show how the whole tenor of society has changed and that homosexuality is now generally regarded as a legitimate lifestyle. Bible-believing Christians can never accept that perspective and so we must accept that we will be treated prejudicially. That should not stop us standing up for biblical teaching, showing love and grace, and seeking every legitimate means to influence the way people think and society conducts itself. However, other legislative changes present an even greater degree of acceptance for practising homosexuals.

EMPLOYMENT EQUALITY (SEXUAL ORIENTATION) REGULATIONS

From 1 December 2003 the Employment Equality (Sexual Orientation) Regulations 2003 made discrimination by employers and trade unions on the ground of sexual orientation unlawful, although discrimination in the provision of public services was not covered. The origin of these Regulations was Article 13 of the Treaty of Amsterdam, which states that, 'Without prejudice to the other provisions of this Treaty and within the limits of the powers conferred by it upon the Community, the Council, acting unanimously on a proposal from the Commission after consulting the European Parliament, may take appropriate action to combat discrimination based on sex, racial or ethnic origin, religion or belief, disability, age or sexual orientation.'

Sexual orientation is defined very broadly to cover heterosexual, homosexual and bisexual relationships. However, the regulations do seek to exclude employees whose sexual preferences may be, for example, sadomasochism or paedophilia. After considerable lobbying churches have been generally exempted, although other areas of Christian activities such as Christian schools and Christian charitable organisations are not. As always in these forms of legislation discrimination is defined under four headings:

- Direct discrimination: refusing a person a job because of their sexual orientation, or treating them less favourably, or disciplining them for issues relevant to their sexual orientation.
- Indirect discrimination: disadvantaging a person in their work situation because of their sexual orientation.
- Harassment: not only is an employer liable for his own conduct, but he may also be liable for the conduct of others if it can be shown that he deliberately put the person in a vulnerable position because of their sexual orientation.
- Victimisation: treating someone, or allowing them to be treated, less favourably because of their sexual orientation.

The principle of genuine occupational requirement (GOR) does apply for recruitment and promotion. The principal area where GOR applies is organised religion. GOR applies where according to regulation 7 of the regulations:

- 'the employment is for purposes of an organised religion;
- the employer applies a requirement related to sexual orientation—so as to comply with the doctrines of the religion, or
- because of the nature of the employment and the context in which it is carried out, so as to avoid conflicting with the strongly held religious convictions of a significant number of the religion's followers; and either—
- the person to whom the requirement is applied does not meet it, or
- the employer is not satisfied, and in all circumstances it is reasonable for him not to be satisfied, that the person meets it.'

There are three areas of concern that arise from this legislation. The first is the situation of Christian organisations whose activities and structure do not directly reflect their religious origins and ethos. It is vital that all Christian organisations maintain and clearly present their religious ethos. To claim to be Christian and yet to follow in every detail the same procedures and practices that a non-Christian organisation in the same area of work would follow is to invite problems. The opportunity and necessity for being distinctively Christian has never been greater. There is no doubt that should Christian organisations live by their Christian ethos they will attract challenge and careful scrutiny. But there is an issue of religious freedom here that must not be shirked or avoided.

A second area of concern is that of Christian managers who work in ordinary employment. There will be situations when in following the legal requirements they may have to implement policies which they cannot personally accept because of the policies' support for a homosexual lifestyle. Similarly, as managers they may have to discipline staff who have breached a code of conduct even when the underlying values of that staff member are the same as their own. The potential for very difficult moral and spiritual dilemmas is real and pastors and church leaders ought to be prepared and informed so that they can support and give guidance to members of their congregations who face these issues.

The third area of concern is discipline of a church employee and the subsequent conduct of church members. It may arise that someone employed by a church who originally met every criterion for the job, including that of sexual orientation, suddenly announces a change of view and the adoption of a homosexual lifestyle. While the church may well be able to invoke its own disciplinary and employment procedures and so dismiss the person, there is a danger of members of the congregation behaving inappropriately and so inviting an accusation of harassment. Where believers behave with love and discretion there is likely to be no problem, but most churches have someone who lacks in these areas to some degree!

GENDER RECOGNITION ACT (2004)

This Bill also poses threats to church life and problems for Christians in their normal working environment. It allows a man to become a woman, even though he still remains physically male, and to change his birth certificate accordingly. Once that change has taken place it would then be legal for the man to marry another man, and so commit homosexual sin. It would also mean that a man may attend a church and require that he be treated as a woman. There was a proscription against someone disclosing the fact of any change which was attended with a substantial fine. That has now been partially ameliorated in regard to membership, marriage and employment in a church. In these situations disclosure is permitted.

The Christian Institute comments, 'There is a concern that the new Gender Recognition Act gives a pretext for litigation against a church. James Dingemans QC shows how the Bill fails to safeguard the rights of religious believers. He concludes that Churches which believe that a transsexual lifestyle is morally wrong are left open to "divisive" legal actions. Although such litigation is ultimately likely to fail, it could be lengthy and costly for Churches. In the past Churches have been sued for refusing a male-to-female transsexual permission to attend ladies' meetings.'[11]

Christians in public service will clearly find themselves in difficulty being required to treat as a woman someone who is in reality a man. In particular, registrars who hold biblical convictions will find themselves in great difficulties. There appears at this time to be little freedom for conscientious objection. This refusal to give adequate recognition to biblical Christianity once more represents the incipient prejudice that pervades our society. Similar problems to those mentioned in regard to the Employment Equality regulations may well arise for managers in the workplace.

CIVIL PARTNERSHIPS BILL

The most dramatic aspect of current legislative changes in terms of its rejection of biblical standards would appear to be the Civil Partnerships Bill. This allows homosexual people who have lived together for two years to register their relationship. There is no doubt that this is a direct attack on the biblical concept of marriage. It is a highly discriminatory piece of legislation. Two members of the same family, e.g. mother and daughter, or two sisters, or two friends living in the same house as co-dependants, or even a live-in carer with a long relationship with the person being cared for, are deliberately excluded from the provisions of the Bill. The 'wrongs' the legislation is seeking to correct as far as homosexuals are concerned are exactly the same as those that apply to these other co-dependants. There are undoubtedly injustices when two people live together in this way, for example, hospital visiting, inheritance, pension rights, property ownership. But this Bill does not seek to deal with the whole spread of injustice; it simply focuses on homosexual couples and their right to register their relationship. Indeed, it goes further in some of its provisions than might have been thought necessary to redress the injustices. That is why so many organisations and lobbying groups have dubbed it 'gay marriage', but that would be quite improper. Whatever a civil partnership is it should not be dignified by calling it a form of marriage.

The implications of this in church life, work, social relationships and even within families are many and varied. That such a Bill could come about with the degree of support it has received once more demonstrates that there is a growing prejudice against the beliefs and values of biblical Christianity.

HOMOPHOBIC HATE LAW

The Government has introduced a Bill to deal with incitement to religious hatred. While this does not strictly refer to the issue of homosexuality, there are aspects of this legislation that do impinge on the subject we are looking at. The chief danger is that this area of law will be expanded and so could lead to further attacks on Christianity within our nation. Already, although using existing legislation, Paul Murphy, Northern Ireland Secretary, has added 'sexual orientation' to racial and religious groups in a schedule of hate crimes which are being prohibited. Indeed, there are those within the homosexual community, with support in Parliament, who want to see a specific crime of 'incitement to homophobic hatred'. So the suggestion that a 'gay humanist' could take legal action against someone propounding biblical views on homosexuality as an incitement to religious hatred is not too far-fetched.

The whole area of freedom of speech is becoming an increasingly vexed one. Cases have arisen where Christians engaging in street preaching have experienced police restriction. This has particularly involved issues surrounding homosexuality. There is an inconsistency here. Whereas the police have used the Public Order Act to curtail freedom of speech on 'content'-based grounds, they have not used that against homosexuals. So a public reading in Central London by Peter Tatchell of a blasphemous poem was permitted with no interference. These trends in the administration of justice merely go to show the general drift within our society against Christian thinking.

The question is increasingly becoming: discrimination against whom?

Responding positively

You can show love without condoning sin. You do not need to reject people because they live in a way that contradicts the teaching of the Bible. You can oppose sin and seek to change people's values without being provocative or aggressive. The trends we have described above, and the changes in the legal framework, should in no way impede Christian activity. God rules over all and the gospel has not been robbed of its power because the British Government has introduced legislation contrary to biblical wisdom. Our whole intellectual framework as Bible-believing Christians takes us beyond the immediate difficulties and challenges of 'post-modern thinking' or 'modern European thought'. We take serious note of the changed environment in which we live but our message need not change one jot.

Since we have the truth from God we must live it out, and speak it out, without fear or favour.

Christians have a clear obligation to keep themselves well informed about all that is happening. Pastors and church leaders need to ensure that they not only know what is going on in the society around but that they also instruct their congregations on how to conduct themselves and how to respond to these challenges. There is a very real need to provide within the framework of the local church's activities support to those in particularly vulnerable areas of work. All these things must complement the earnest praying of God's people, and the consistent and urgent preaching of the gospel.

HOMOPHOBIA

One thing that is certain in the present climate is that faithful Christians will be accused of 'homophobia'. This term tends to be used very widely and sometimes inadvisedly. The origins of the word are interesting.

As western society rethought its whole approach to sexual orientation, opposition to homosexuality was crystallised in the term homophobia, which heterosexual psychologist George Weinberg coined in the late 1960s. Weinberg used homophobia to label heterosexuals' dread of being in close quarters with homosexuals as well as homosexuals' self-loathing. The word first appeared in print in 1969 and was subsequently discussed at length in Weinberg's 1972 book *Society and the Healthy Homosexual.*

The American Heritage Dictionary (1992 edition) defines homophobia as 'aversion to gay or homosexual people or their lifestyle or culture' and 'behaviour or an act based on this aversion'. Other definitions identify homophobia as an irrational fear of homosexuality. So the online dictionary AskOxford.com (which is in effect the Compact Oxford English Dictionary) defines it as 'an extreme and irrational aversion to homosexuality and homosexuals'. The concept of irrationality is surely significant. The Christian position is not irrational, nor is it a fear. We do have an aversion to the lifestyle, culture and value system of practising homosexuals, but we love them as we love all other people, and we object to their ideas on the basis of revealed faith not unthought-out fears.

The accusation and name-calling involved in the use of the word 'homophobia' should not be a discouragement to any Christian who is being faithful to the Bible and is conducting himself with Christian grace and love. The fear of evangelical Christians exhibited by those who constantly cry 'homophobia' where there is no 'homophobia' is an evidence of their deliberate denial of God and his word.

CHRISTIANS IN THE WORKPLACE

Some of the issues that will affect Christians in their work have already been raised. In certain areas of work and for those holding positions of authority there could be specific problems that will arise as the legal and cultural bias towards homosexuals conflicts with personal convictions. This is not a new situation. With rose-coloured spectacles we can look back on some halcyon day when everyone held Christian values. But it never really existed. Consistent Bible-believers have always found themselves at odds with the prevailing culture. We must, therefore, continue to do what Christians have always done—live godly and caring lives before all men.

Of course, we must also realise that much of the legislation we have been discussing does give Christians the right to hold their views provided they do so without giving offence or appearing to discriminate against those with whom we disagree. Equal opportunity policy statements will generally define the rights and expectations that are placed on all employees. Christians should know their position accurately and conduct themselves with wisdom. That is really a straightforward matter. Above all else, in the event of an issue arising that really affects Christian faith and obedience, it is a privilege to suffer for Christ. The early church rejoiced when they were 'counted worthy to suffer shame for his name' (Acts 4:41).

ISSUES IN EDUCATION

Christian Unions in universities and colleges may well be put under greater pressures as they express the biblical perspective on homosexuality. Nonetheless, they should not bend, but with grace and wisdom they should continue to present the gospel and to establish young Christians in the faith of Jesus Christ. The support given by the Christian Institute to Hull University Christian Union shows that with grace and wisdom righteousness can be maintained. Here is a matter for serious prayer by Christians throughout the country.

SOCIAL ACTION

Christian societies working across the whole field of social welfare have a great opportunity to display the distinctiveness of Christian values in our morally uncertain age. Christians in general need to review the societies they support and ensure that those which are striving to maintain a biblical witness receive the fullest backing. What more impressive way is there of seeking to redress the errors of the past, and of showing the essential values of Christian truth than by ministering to those from the homosexual community when they face need and hardship? Churches also have an opportunity to reach out to homosexuals with love and compassion, seeking to avoid that spirit of judgementalism which has so often hindered effective ministry.

People who have chosen a homosexual lifestyle face the same challenges in life that everyone else does; indeed in some areas of life they face greater difficulties because of the nature of their lifestyle. Here is the opportunity to reflect the love of Christ and to reach out hands of friendship and concern to them. Nothing will dispel prejudice in individuals more quickly than acts of love and care.

It is also vital that Christians take seriously the need to support campaigning groups like the Christian Institute and CARE as they present to politicians and the general public the biblical perspective on the issues we have been considering.

Christian thinking and living

The pre-eminent challenge to every evangelical Christian is simply to think and live as Christians should. 'Let your light so shine before men, that they may see your good works and glorify your Father in heaven' (Matthew 5:16).

Notes

1 Introduction to a model equal opportunities policy produced by **Age Concern England** (February 1997).
2 **Don A. Carson,** *The Gagging of God* (Apollos, 1996), p. 32.
3 Ibid. p. 32.
4 **William Rees-Mogg,** *The Times* (London), 26 October 2004.

5　**The Christian Institute,** News Update 1997, no. 2, quoting **Robert H. Knight,** *New NIX Study Indicates Homosexuality Is Learned,* Family Research Council; also King and MacDonald study 1992 referred to in **Jeffrey Satinover,** *Homosexuality and the Politics of Truth* (Grand Rapids: Baker Book House, 1995).

6　*Between the Lines,* 12 August 2004, reprinted on the Independent Gay Forum: www.indegayforum.org/authors/corvino/corvino9.html

7　www.care.org.uk

8　**Don A. Carson,** *op. cit.,* p.422.

9　**The Christian Institute,** Wilberforce House, 4 Park Road, Gosforth Business Park, Newcastle-upon-Tyne NE12 8DG, tel: 0191 281 5664, fax: 0191 2814272, www.christian.org.uk

10　*Demolishing Arguments,* The Christian Institute Annual Review 2002–2003, p.13.

11　**The Christian Institute,** *Institute Update,* Issue 5, August 2004.

Pastoral response in the local church

Declan Flanagan

Picking up the telephone is often an invitation to journey into the unknown. 'I must see you quickly. This is important and cannot be talked about over the telephone.' The sense of anxiety in the voice indicated that there was little time to waste. A meeting was hastily arranged with a young man intending to inform his parents and church that he was homosexual.

In the next few days I was forced to re-examine what the Bible has to say about homosexuality. I also had the opportunity to learn a great deal about the tensions that a homosexually-orientated person faces. The young man was clear that his homosexual orientation was not a choice he was exercising. His desire was not to be attracted to someone of the same sex and the sense of guilt was deeply troubling. We prayed together and read everything available.

Eventually the announcement to the church was never made, and several years later the person concerned would declare he still has to combat temptation towards same-sex relationships. However, his perspective on himself and on his sexuality is no longer the same. He has a new sense of security in his relationship with Christ. Instead of being tormented by guilt, he shows evidence of personal fulfilment and genuine freedom.

Since then I have had conversations with both men and women seeking guidance about homosexuality, bisexuality and what to do if you are married to a homosexual. Each person is different and there is much to learn from them. Some have strong desires for God and seek to be part of a worshipping community. To share their struggles has been a privilege and much of what is included in this chapter arises from our conversations and study together of the Bible. Several have read and made helpful comments about this chapter. You will not find a simple 'five steps to follow' approach;

someone seeking help does not want to encounter a formula, but a person with whom they can relate.

Churches sometimes struggle with complexity and find categorising people convenient. Since how we label or identify people often defines them, we must avoid reducing someone to one aspect of their identity, which can be dehumanising. Only seeing someone in relation to their sexuality fails to appreciate other aspects of the person concerned. Complexity exists in seeking to find reasons for same-sex attraction. There is a growing body of evidence pointing to the influence of genetic, brain structure and/or hormonal factors as being significant in the development of homosexual orientation. There continues to be much that is unknown.[1]

Understanding yourself

My first conversations with someone indicating they were homosexual brought to the surface many inner attitudes and questions that could not be ignored. As a hot-blooded man who grew up in a sporting environment, I know what it is to struggle with lust for women. No member of the football club I belonged to had ever found an inoculation that made us immune from sexual temptation. We were fiercely heterosexual in orientation and someone declaring himself as homosexual would be given a very hard time. Among us there was a profound distaste at any suggestion of same-sex activity. We were sure that homosexual men would be unmarried and could be expected to display limp wrists, swivel hips, feminine clothing and affected speech. It would have been impossible to think, at that stage, of inviting a known homosexual to play the role of a hard-tackling full back. Homosexual women were a little more difficult to spot, but short-cropped-hair, baggy trousers and Dr Martens boots might give some indication. Certainly we would not have expected a lesbian to be the stunning woman who would accompany one of the lads for a night out.

Our understanding of homosexuality conformed to media stereotypes and personal reactions indicated a lack of any serious consideration of the issue. I was decidedly ignorant. The notion that outward appearance or speech indicate if someone is homosexual is widespread, but they are not accurate indicators. The only way to be sure is if someone tells you of their sexual orientation.

My background, coupled with some early Christian influences that suggested anything to do with sex inevitably must be unholy, meant I was not in a good position to help people considering their sexual orientation. Our inner attitudes must be appreciated and examined. All of us can be tempted to use Scripture to confirm our own preferences and prejudices. When we do this, we abuse the Bible and are unable to assist those who may make themselves vulnerable enough to speak to us. If they are met with hostility and anger that comes from our background and prejudices, it is likely that only one conversation will take place. A fearful anticipation of rejection can be one of the contributory factors that lead people into an active homosexual lifestyle. The gay community will claim they can offer understanding and support, while the church is more likely to offer misunderstanding and condemnation. If we can manage to think ourselves into someone else's situation and realise their vulnerability, we will be aware of the danger of communicating a sense of rejection. It is a privilege to be allowed to share the deepest thoughts and feelings of someone else.

Any human being, regardless of sexual orientation, has the same basic need to love and be loved. Through the grace of God we can find the resources of patience, kindness and a love that is not easily angered, but protects, trusts, hopes and perseveres. To some I have apologised for unhelpful comments or premature conclusions.

Homosexuality is just one of a whole range of human weaknesses, from which Christians are not immune. If somebody seeks help with alcoholism, drug addiction, gambling, anorexia or other issues, we would be prepared to speak supportively with them. Homosexuality should not be regarded as a special case. Any pastor after several years of ministry could compile a book detailing particular difficulties that have been considered with Christians. If published it would surely be a bestseller.

Know and declare the truth

With messages advocating the legitimacy of intimate homosexual relationships being promoted with such regularity, we need to have a clear understanding of what Scripture says about same-sex relationships. The Bible is definite in saying that homosexual practice is a sin. With clarity and compassion we must uphold God's standards.

Specific Bible references are dealt with more fully in other places within this book and it is essential to be well acquainted with them. These passages will probably have been studied, in depth, by Christians declaring themselves to be homosexual. Rather than entering into a heated debate on particular texts, I have found it helpful to be aware of the whole doctrinal framework that indicates homosexual practice to be wrong. This understanding has governed my pastoral practice. In the three New Testament passages where Paul writes about homosexuality, what is most impressive is his understanding of the character and purposes of God (Romans 1:26–27; 1 Corinthians 6:9–11; 1 Timothy 1:9–11).

In Romans 1 it is the *doctrine of creation* that undergirds the argument against homosexual practice. The whole chapter underlines the fact that we are spiritually and morally in rebellion against the Creator's design. All homosexual behaviour is wrong, along with lots of other things, including deceit, arrogance, disobedience and that frequently excused sin of gossip.

Paul reasons that homosexuality clashes with God's intention for human sexuality, whatever individual homosexuals feel about the 'naturalness' of their orientation. It is not God's plan for the expression of our sexuality. Since the Fall, sin has damaged us all. Homosexuality is not a sign of God's order for creation but of fallen disorder. This is contrary to the view advanced by Rev. Richard Kirker, secretary of the Lesbian and Gay Christian Movement: 'It would be a very cavalier and capricious God who created people in a certain way and then instructed them that they are forbidden from fulfilling all the potential they have been given.'[2] The potential that Richard Kirker is referring to is the potential for homosexual activity. The lack of understanding of the creation and the Fall leads to a rejection of both celibacy and chastity, for those with either a heterosexual or homosexual orientation.

In 1 Corinthians 6 the attention shifts to what it means to live in *God's kingdom* and be subject to the Lord Jesus Christ. Some behaviour, of which homosexuality is referred to as just one example, is incompatible with life under God's rule.

In 1 Timothy 1:10 Paul highlights the *law of God* as he gives an updated version of the ten commandments. Homosexual intercourse is bracketed with heterosexual adultery: both are 'contrary to sound doctrine, in accordance with the glorious gospel of the blessed God'.

So the arguments against homosexual practice are not found in random texts dealing with cultural issues far removed from life as we know it today. There is an impressive biblical chain involving God who reveals himself as Creator, King and Lawgiver. In God's plan for human life, from creation to the coming of his kingdom, homosexual behaviour has no place. This understanding is held by the vast majority of evangelical churches. Ninety-six per cent of churches linked with the Evangelical Alliance believe homosexual sex to be wrong. Clive Calver writes that 'the vast numbers of churches stand by 2,000 years of biblical analysis which conclude that homosexual sex is outside the will and purpose of God'.[3]

God has created people with all sorts of potentials, including the potential to disobey his laws. Both heterosexuals and homosexuals have a 'potential' for sexual activity. God declares that the correct place for that potential to be realised is within the context of heterosexual marriage. God's standards are not irrational or cruel burdens; they are for our benefit.

Understanding what the Bible teaches about homosexual behaviour is not an end to the discussion about the way individuals or the church should relate to gay and lesbian people. If I am to love my neighbour, and my neighbour is a practising homosexual, how do I do that? When your child or a close Christian friend declares that they are in an active homosexual relationship, what do you do? Being well acquainted with the Bible's teaching is an important starting point, but it is really only a beginning. Simply quoting texts at people is like a police officer's hand indicating 'Stop!' without pointing to an alternative, better way.

Having sought both to clarify and communicate the Bible's teaching, it is possible to develop a pastoral strategy.

Acknowledge the difficulties

Part of the difficulty evangelicals have in ministering effectively to homosexuals is that we may want to find quick and easy solutions to complex issues. The perception is often that the evangelical church has stood with Moses on Mount Sinai hurling down the commandments. Probably unknown to many both inside and outside of the church is the significant number of men and women who have received compassionate care.

The homosexually-orientated person knows that their feelings are real, that they are deep-seated and probably have been unspoken for many years. They are unlikely to have woken up one day and decided to rebel against God and become a homosexual. No exhortation to pray more, to be more Spirit-filled, or to be more of anything is likely to immediately change the situation.

How many people within our churches are struggling with a tendency towards same-sex relationships? The best research in the United States discovered the percentage of homosexual men in the population to be 3·7%.4 I have seen no accurate studies giving figures for women attracted to the same sex. Some writers have estimated the figures to be lower and others to be slightly higher. I see no reason to suggest that a figure of around 4% would not be found in the majority of churches. People are unlikely to wear badges identifying themselves and sadly many are unprepared to speak to another Christian or a church leader. New Christians and many younger people are much more open in sharing their difficulties. They consider that keeping silent on controversial issues is an indicator of superficial relationships and a 'let's bury our heads in the sand' syndrome.

Where there is a general silence on sexual matters, it leaves those facing same-sex temptations with many questions. Is it better to remain silent? How do you effectively combat temptation and discouragement on your own? Is it right to take communion? Will I be subject to church discipline for my orientation? Should someone remain in the church and confide in a friend or church leader? Is it better to stay in the church but seek help from elsewhere? Would it be better to move on to another church that is known for its acceptance of homosexuals but does not have the same understanding of the Bible? Does the desire for honesty in relationships mean that significant factors should be disclosed? How does anyone face the potential of rejection and misunderstanding in their lives?

These and other questions are not imaginary. I have been asked each one.

Challenge the lies
Two of the greatest deceptions that Satan has managed to sow are that

'whatever you feel, you are', and 'if it feels good, do it'. Restraint is regarded as repressive today and sexual experimentation is openly encouraged, without any thought of the consequences. The problem with distortions of truth is that they appear so plausible, offering freedom not tyranny. They also ignore the fallen state of human nature. We were all born with a corrupt nature that is full of all kinds of evil desires. If everyone gave way to their base instincts, the world would know even greater pain and chaos. Is it being true to oneself to give way to every ungodly lust, however natural it may feel? Is the unmarried person free to become sexually involved with anyone they find attractive? Is the married person free to commit adultery because they are drawn to someone else and they should not deny themselves?

A significant view in our society is that sexual desire should not be restrained in any way. 'Everyone should be free to do as they choose,' is the argument. Those aware of Judges 21:25, where 'everyone did what was right in his own eyes', will know that this is not a recent understanding. What is false is the assumption that everyone has to have a sexual relationship in order to be fulfilled. The Christian way is different. Paul writes that 'the grace of God that brings salvation has appeared to all men. It teaches us to say "No" to ungodliness and worldly passions, and to live self-controlled, upright and godly lives in this present age' (Titus 2:11–12, NIV). A vital part of Christian living is to be aware of what are right and wrong desires. There is a higher authority than our feelings and desires— what God has declared to be right or wrong.

Understand the varieties of sexual orientations

Labels are dangerous and frequently misleading. Some people believe there are only two types of sexual orientation: heterosexual where a person is attracted to members of the opposite sex, and homosexual where a person is sexually attracted to members of the same sex. This is a limited understanding because it ignores other groups. Asexuals are people who feel attracted to neither gender. Bisexuals find themselves attracted to both genders, often in different degrees.

Appreciating the sexual orientation of a person is an important step to understanding the individual and the particular issues they face. Many researchers into human sexuality look upon sexual orientation as a continuum and certainly not as something fixed during adolescence.

Follow the Lord's example

Should a notorious sinner enter a room, how would you react? What do you really think when you hear for the first time that someone is a homosexual? Would your tendency be to confront or avoid them? Is the issue of their homosexuality so large that you cannot see the person? How do you think Jesus would react?

In an account unique to Luke (7:36–50), a woman living an unspecified immoral life disturbed a well-ordered dinner party at the home of Simon the Pharisee. She is not reported as saying anything, but her actions provoked some strong opinions. Adultery was as big an issue in the time of Jesus as homosexuality is today. People had firm and fixed ideas of what punishment was appropriate. The way in which Jesus handled the situation provides a good model of how to minister to those who know their lives are affected by sin and who seek the Lord's help. Jesus did not dismiss but welcomed her. In the face of opposition, very publicly, he offered her support.

The significance of the actions and words of Jesus were not lost on those attending the dinner. They were aware of the Old Testament expression of abhorrence of prostitution, homosexuality and any form of immorality. Jesus had the power to forgive sins and told the woman to 'go in peace'. In doing so, he stood in stark contrast to the Pharisees. Jesus said to another group who wanted his opinion on whether a woman caught in adultery should be stoned: 'If any one of you is without sin, let him be the first to throw a stone at her' (John 8:7, NIV).

I do not find it difficult to identify with the attitudes of the Pharisees. Whether it is adultery or homosexual practice, it is easier to condemn than to have the attitude of Christ and follow his example. Certainly where sin is involved, Jesus is uncompromising. The woman caught in adultery is told to 'go, and from now on sin no more' (John 8:11). Jesus would not agree that anything done in the name of 'love' is acceptable. In the discussion about long-term homosexual relationships, it is quickly forgotten that Jesus said, 'If you love me, you will keep my commandments' (John 14:15).

In his dealings with people, Jesus conveyed with clarity that sin is wrong, whether in thought or action. However, he always welcomed sinners and was consistently compassionate. This balance is far from easy to maintain. It is the example of our Lord we should seek to imitate, not modern-day Pharisees.

Distinguish between temptation and sin

Is it a sin to feel attracted to someone of the same sex? Does God condemn you for those feelings? Is it all right to fantasise but not become actively involved?

Questions such as these indicate the need for careful thought. There is no getting away from temptation. The devil has greater skill than any advertising agencies. He knows our weak spots and will tempt continuously.

Sexual temptation is part of being human and all Christians have to deal with inappropriate sexual feelings and attractions. Those tempted to homosexual activity are not members of a sub-group within the Christian community. It is helpful to appreciate that the word temptation is neutral. God has no part in directing us towards evil. 'When tempted, no-one should say, "God is tempting me." For God cannot be tempted by evil, nor does he tempt anyone; but each one is tempted when, by his own evil desire, he is dragged away and enticed' (James 1:13–14, NIV).

There is a difference between being tempted and falling. Jesus was tempted in every way, 'just as we are—yet was without sin' (Hebrews 4:15, NIV). Temptation is like someone knocking on your door. At times the intensity of the knocking is deafening; other times it is a little quieter. Sin is opening the door and making it possible for the tempter to enter. Being sexually attracted to another person is not the same as committing adultery in your heart (Matthew 5:28). It becomes sin when you respond to the temptation in either mind or body. Part of the difficulty in dealing with sexual lust is that we say 'yes' too quickly and 'no' too slowly.

Temptation gives way to sin through a process of enticement. There is always a time-gap between conception and birth. An improper desire for heterosexual or homosexual sex, occurring in the mind, can be either killed or nurtured. When, for example, a heterosexual man sees an attractive woman walking down the street, sexual attraction is his likely response. Unless he is to keep his eyes closed (and risk the danger of walking into a lamp-post), the situation is largely unavoidable. A choice has to be made either to resist the temptation or to develop fantasies about the woman. The results of that choice determine whether or not he has entered into the sin of lust.

When the person of a homosexual orientation is tempted, the same principles are operative. If every time we experienced hunger we felt a deep-seated guilt, we would be in trouble. Hunger is not gluttony and sexual temptation, in whatever form, is not specific sin. Sin occurs when we permit our thoughts to grow into lust and when we desire what is not rightfully ours.

Failure to distinguish between temptation and sin leads to unnecessary guilt and a sense of inevitable failure. Every temptation is an opportunity to come closer to God and for his power to be displayed in your life. When the tempter's incessant knocking on the door of your life wears you down to the point of despair, you must know what to do. Do not open the door. Better still, remind the tempter that Jesus Christ has taken up residence and is now in charge.

Michael Saia writes a word of warning about seeing temptation to homosexual sin as the only difficulty:

> Homosexually orientated men often believe that their temptation to homosexual sin is their biggest problem. During counseling they discover there are other weaknesses in their lives that pose far greater challenges than the temptation to homosexuality. Men frequently comment to me that if they are controlling certain other problems, the temptation to homosexual sin is easier to resist.[5]

Women attracted to other women are often concerned about loneliness and a lack of friends during adolescence. A sense of inferiority and self-pity may lead to an insatiable desire to find an ideal woman figure. When other significant factors are acknowledged, it helps avoid concentrating solely on homosexuality.

Develop a carefully considered approach

Sadly, those who are prepared to seek help may encounter ill-conceived, unhelpful responses. For many Christians the immediate reaction following disclosure of a homosexual orientation or lifestyle is to pray for immediate healing and seek help from someone with a ministry of deliverance. While there is much to be gained through prayer and sensitive biblical counselling, to pursue holiness of life must be the primary goal. Some may think that as a result of ministry or counselling the indicator of a changed sexual orientation will be a desire for marriage. Expectations must be in keeping with the overall teaching of the Bible. Not all temptation is put away to the extent that it never has the potential to reappear. It is evident that not all who are physically sick are healed.

God's desire for us is not constant personal fulfilment without any difficulties, but holiness. The instruction in 1 Peter 1:15–16 is not specifically for homosexuals, but for all: 'But as he who called you is holy, you also be holy in all your conduct, since it is written: "You shall be holy, for I am holy."' We aim for wholeness and restoration from the consequences of the Fall, which have different manifestations, in order to become like Christ. Any development of a holy life is slow and painful, with many disappointments along the way.

Paul was in no doubt that change is possible in any area of our lives. He wrote that among the Christians at Corinth were those who were formerly idolaters, male prostitutes, homosexual offenders, thieves and swindlers. 'And such were some of you. But you were washed, you were sanctified, you were justified in the name of the Lord Jesus Christ and by the Spirit of our God' (1 Corinthians 6:10–11).

Immense pressure can be placed on someone if the primary objective of counselling or pastoral care is seen to be a change in sexual orientation. As the life of Christ develops through the work of the Holy Spirit, people cannot remain the same. Where there is a deeply embedded belief that change is impossible, this can give way to a conviction that nothing is impossible with God. His touch has the potential to bring healing to specific areas of our life affected by sin and this can have a profound effect on our whole well-being. Where a woman may have experienced sexual abuse, he can bring release from a hatred of men. Forgiveness for those who have caused harm through actions or critical words becomes possible.

There are Christians who indicate that they find little change in their sexual orientation but that the grace of God is sufficient to keep them from sinful actions and relationships. We will have to wait until heaven for absolute wholeness and some aspects of our sinful nature continue to cause all of us problems. We need to be constantly on our guard. Some become aware that their sexuality is not static and either that heterosexual attraction is already present or starts to develop. For those who may be married, Lori Rentzel writes a word of caution. She experienced periods of strong sexual and emotional attraction to women. She writes:

never again will I view my sexuality as set in stone. Not a year goes by where I do not question, examine and pray about some aspect of what it means to be a woman and uncover some new area of my sexuality that needs healing or redefining. As a mother of three small daughters, I have added motivation for discovering and embracing God's full intent for me as a woman.[6]

In order to grow in Christ and have the power to resist temptation, it is imperative that we use the means God has provided. The following areas may be helpfully explored by someone with a homosexual orientation or lifestyle and those who seek to befriend them.

APPRECIATE THE CHARACTER OF GOD

Something is wrong with the church in our culture today. Many people want a God of 'love' as they define it. They don't want the biblical God of love, whose love is inseparable from his justice, holiness and righteousness. The light of God is in no way incompatible with his love. As we come to know the different aspects of God's character we appreciate his holiness as well as his love. We bow before his majesty and thank him for his faithfulness. Confidence grows as we remember that God is just and that the difficulties we face with living in a fallen world are not what he intended for us. God's mercy and forgiveness are available to those who know they fail. He longs to help in the daily circumstances of life. He shares our pains, rejoices in our victories and delights to answer prayer.

FIND YOUR SECURITY IN CHRIST

Wondering about our identity and being over-concerned about who approves or disapproves of us leads to insecurity. Knowledge at a deep personal level that we are very precious earthly children of our heavenly

Father will take time to develop. We need to learn to think of ourselves in the way the Bible describes us. As we see ourselves as God sees us, we become less conscious of how others view us. Trusting God with our past, present and future involves faith in what Christ has done and is able to do for us.

GROW IN HONESTY

Honesty with God and ourselves is essential. Many are drawn into active homosexual relationships for social or emotional reasons. If the reasons are not predominantly sexual, what are they? How can they be met apart from a homosexual relationship? Has an attempt been made to justify what is known to be wrong?

DEAL SPECIFICALLY WITH SIN

In churches with little emphasis on God's character and law, people who have little conviction of sin may be encouraged to come to Christ. Jesus Christ is not seen as the Saviour from sin, but as the one who is there for our benefit and who will help us in times of difficulty. When old problems do not quickly go away, it is easy to be disappointed and blame Christ for the lack of success. Any lack of conviction of sin in the beginning always leads to weakness as time goes by. It is always important to check what understanding of repentance someone has in order to discern if there is evidence of a relationship with God.

Practising homosexuals often regret their lifestyles and feel sorry for the way they are living but are not prepared to call their actions sinful. Where sin is involved there is no forgiveness without acknowledgement. King David, who struggled with sexual sin, knew the essential link between repentance and forgiveness. 'I acknowledged my sin to you, and I did not cover my iniquity. I said, "I will confess my transgressions to the LORD"— and you forgave the iniquity of my sin' (Psalm 32:5).

A loathing of sin needs to develop in order to be free from it. 'If I had cherished iniquity in my heart, the Lord would not have listened' (Psalm 66:18). Someone is deceived if they think they can have all the benefits of the Christian life while continuing to sin. Breaking known sinful patterns of behaviour and replacing them with new ones will be one of the marks of genuine repentance.

The old sinful nature has an insatiable desire for attention and cries out all the more when it senses any deprivation. Christ provides the power to resist temptation and develop new attitudes. That power is linked to the cross where Christ suffered and died for all our sins. There are times when we do sin, but that does not mean we have to live forever under condemnation. After repenting of our sin and asking forgiveness, we need to get on with living. Wallowing in self-pity or thinking that there is no hope may well be an indication of preoccupation with self.

SELF-CONTROL IS ESSENTIAL

Self-control is a gift of the Spirit, one of the fruits of the Spirit but also a command to be obeyed (Titus 2:11–15; 2 Peter 1:5–6). There is no difference in this requirement for either heterosexual or homosexual-orientated Christian people.

WATCH AND PRAY

This command was given by the Lord to his disciples shortly before he went to the cross. In the garden of Gethsemane he experienced a long and painful struggle concerning his future. He warned the disciples that if they did not want to be led into temptation, they must watch and pray.

Watching suggests a soldier on guard, alert for the first sign of enemy attack. We watch against temptation by noticing what situations, company and influences are likely to lead us into sin. It was Martin Luther who said, 'You can't stop the birds flying over your head, but you can stop them nesting in your hair.' Preventative strategies have to be arranged. There is a battle to engage in and the way Jesus resisted Satan in the desert indicates the necessity of knowing and using the word of God (Luke 4:1–13). Paul writes 'do not be conformed to this world, but be transformed by the renewal of your mind' (Romans 12:2). Regular patterns of Bible reading have an impact on our thought patterns and help us to resist temptation.

The kind of intensity of prayer that took place in Gethsemane is a good model to help in times of difficulty. We too can pray for strength to do what we know to be right in the face of an inward reluctance to do so. Thanksgiving and praise help put our difficulties into perspective and stop us concentrating on ourselves. Many have found keeping a diary or journal that honestly records successes and failures to be helpful. This can include prayers to God expressing how we really feel.

RELATE TO THE REST OF THE CHRISTIAN FAMILY

For many homosexual people this is a particularly difficult area. Regrettably a homosexual person will not find the same love and understanding in the church as they will receive from the heavenly Father. Churches need to consider how they relate to someone tempted by or involved in same-sex relationships. Will they find more understanding in the 'gay community' than among Christ's community? John Stott writes, 'At the heart of the homosexual condition is a deep loneliness, the natural human hunger for mutual love, a search for identity and a longing for completeness. If homosexual people cannot find these things in the local church family, we have no business to go on using that expression.'7

We all need friends with whom we can share our deepest thoughts. Isolation and inactivity present their own particular difficulties. Bearing each other's burdens allows us to talk about difficult issues, without fear, embarrassment or rejection. This may mean trusting a church leader or small group with matters that you agree should remain confidential. It is not necessary or helpful for someone to disclose their sexual temptations to the whole church.

While we all have a need for close, same-sex friendships, it is advisable to have several close friends of both sexes in order to avoid damaging emotional and dependent relationships. This is particularly important for lesbians who have been involved in 'all or nothing' relationships that have been very intense. Non-sexual relationships allow love to be given and received in ways that are enhancing for all involved.

In urging abstinence from sexual relationships, except within marriage, any church must be prepared to actively encourage an environment of love, acceptance and support. A right desire to uphold God's standards must accompany a spirit of humility and gentleness (Galatians 6:1).

BE STRONG IN THE LORD

Before bringing together his teaching on spiritual warfare, Paul has a word of exhortation: 'Finally, be strong in the Lord and in the strength of his might' (Ephesians 6:10). He is well aware that our enemy is powerful, clever and experienced. He has a great ally in what the Bible calls the 'flesh'—that conglomeration of ungodly lusts and selfishness which we will have with us until death. In our own strength we will fail constantly. Through the strength of the Lord nothing is impossible.

WHEN A PARENT HEARS THEIR CHILD IS HOMOSEXUAL

On being informed that their child is attracted to someone of the same sex, or is homosexually active, parents will face conflicting emotions. These may include shock, guilt, shame and acute disappointment. Fears may arise concerning the potential lack of grandchildren or death through Aids. A surge of emotions and unanswered questions can result in parental love being submerged under a tidal wave of anger and rejection. Condemnation is probably the biggest enemy to someone with a homosexual orientation and has the potential to drive them away.

Your child is still your child and is not so much seeking your approval as your love. God's love still reaches us if we have sinned, and parental love needs to reach out towards the child even if homosexual sin is involved. A child's disclosure concerning their sexuality must not obliterate the many joys you have shared in the past. The decision by a child to speak about deep-seated personal issues is usually a token of trust in parents. They have been prepared to make themselves completely vulnerable. No parent can live their life through their children and what they desperately want to know is whether you love them with no strings attached.

Love in the Bible is primarily an action and love for a child needs to be demonstrated at every possible opportunity. Parents, brothers and sisters and other relatives all have an important part to play. God's grace is available to those with conflicting emotions. He can give patience and help to resist the temptation of trying to sort this matter out in twenty-four hours.

As parents ask, 'Why our child?' and 'Is it our fault?' it is helpful to make contact with others who have faced similar difficulties. A trusted church leader may be able to assist. Hurting parents need support from other Christians and this cannot be received if nobody is told. There is always pain in disclosure, but there is greater pain in bearing burdens alone.

Many parents have very little knowledge of homosexuality and will need to discover from good Christian literature as much as possible in a short time. This will help in understanding the child better and in appreciating the complex issues involved. All children have their needs, dreams, desires, problems, faults, failures and sins. It can be hard for parents to realise that children are just as human as they are.

Summary

People are complex: not only is our self-understanding limited, but we find it difficult to understand others. Someone will have sacrificed a great deal by sharing their deepest thoughts. We must be careful in listening and avoid the trap of thinking that all homosexual issues and relationships are the same.

To commence a conversation with the subject of 'sin' is likely to add to an existing sense of rejection and isolation. What is required is genuine Christian love that appreciates and cares. Immediate support and encouragement for those with a homosexual orientation are required rather than censure. It is in this context that growth towards wholeness in Christ can be furthered and sinful attitudes and actions addressed. Maintaining contact over a long period of time will be enormously helpful. This permits opportunity to develop temptation resistance strategies and accountability relationships. For those who may be married but are tempted to same-sex relationships, I urge honesty within marriage and regular, honest meetings with trusted friends.

The easy access to internet pornography and chat rooms has enormously increased pressures in recent years. I warmly recommend finding www.covenanteyes.com and inviting a trusting friend to check internet access trails.

Where churches are unable or unwilling to attempt to minister to homosexual people, contact with specific Christian ministries will be required. Such ministries have a valuable part to play in not only helping individuals but educating the wider church.

There are homosexual people outside of our churches open to the gospel of Christ. We need to see them and be prepared to love them, as Christ does. Where we have failed to do so, repentance is required. Homosexuality is not an unwelcome issue that is best swept under the carpet. If we do this,

Christians seeking guidance and support will be swept right out of the doors of evangelical churches. In preaching and teaching programmes it is time to break any conspiracy of silence that exists concerning human sexuality. Failure to speak clearly and honestly allows secular voices to remain unchallenged. Preaching should refer to the wide variety of sexual sins recorded in Scripture. Examples of God's grace and comfort to people who struggle with brokenness are very helpful. Church leaders need to teach about homosexuality and provide definite suggestions on how to minister to people, inside and outside of the church. Celibacy should not be portrayed as being given the booby prize. It has a long and positive tradition extending back to Christ himself.

Temptation is something that affects us all in various ways and the Bible tells us how to avoid falling into sin. The way we do that is the same for those tempted to homosexual or heterosexual sin. Sin does not have to master us. The resources to combat sin are powerful: the Holy Spirit within us; the word of God in our hearts and on our lips; the blood of Christ speaking of our justification and cleansing and Christian friends who will stand with us. We have a good news message to proclaim to heterosexual and homosexual sinners.

Notes

1 See a helpful chapter in **David K. Switzer,** *Pastoral Care of Gays, Lesbians and Their Families* (Fortress Press, 1999).

2 **Richard Kirker,** Interview with **Paul Vallely** in *The Independent*, 11 November 1996.

3 **Clive Calver,** *Idea Magazine*, Evangelical Alliance, January-March 1997, p. 31.

4 **Joseph Harry,** 'A Probability Sample of Gay Males', *Journal of Homosexuality* 19, 1990, p. 96.

5 **Michael Saia,** *Counseling the Homosexual* (Minneapolis: Bethany House, 1988), p. 149.

6 **Lori Rentzel** writing in *Striving for gender identity* (German Institute of Youth and Society), p. 202.

7 **John Stott,** *Issues facing Christians today* (Marshalls, 1984), p. 231.

8 **Norman Fraser,** *The Net Commandments* (Leicester: IVP, 2002), provides helpful reading.

Martin's story

Martin Hallett

This chapter consists almost entirely of extracts from Martin Hallett's book *Still Learning to Love* (HOW Publications, 2004), by kind permission.

Early days

I often felt drawn to other boys and the younger masters at school, especially anyone good at sport. One of my best friends, Tony, was an active sportsman and often encouraged me to play more effectively. I never really enjoyed sport or was successful at it; I mostly joined in to be accepted. Many times I would see Tony and his friends with their arms around each other. I longed for him to relate to me like that—but he did not.

Even the teacher I admired seemed to be playfully affectionate with other boys, but not with me. Someone announced that people who liked men more than women were homosexuals. I found myself blushing because it seemed to describe the way I felt. In fact I could remember having a 'crush' on Richard Burton and Laurence Harvey, whom I met through my brother when I was only seven. Now, at thirteen, I found a book at home on sexuality and read that boys go through a homosexual stage. It crossed my mind that I might grow out of these feelings, although I was not totally convinced this would happen. Sexual activity with other boys was out of the question for me. I am not sure I even wanted it very much; it seemed 'dirty'.

College life was far less disciplined than school and it was not long before I was taking advantage of this. It was at this time that I discovered a place in Liverpool, near my bus-stop, where homosexuals met for sexual relationships. There was no social contact, it was simply a place for importuning. I was fascinated, but too shy to get involved. If I missed my train in the morning I would spend the day wandering around Birkenhead or Liverpool, hanging around places I knew homosexual men met for sex (I never actually met anyone for sex). Then I would arrive home at the normal time. My sexuality was certainly developing now and I knew I was definitely interested in men. However, I found it difficult to believe that they would be interested in me until I was older, because at sixteen my voice had still not broken. A fascination with the male physique encouraged me to start buying bodybuilding magazines, which were supposedly for athletic interest, but I think were really produced for homosexuals. They were the equivalent of 'girlie' magazines. This was before the days of blatant homosexual pornography but, nevertheless, interest in these magazines soon became something of an addiction. I used to hide them at home, but I know my mother discovered them at various times, although nothing was ever said. I guess she must have been very concerned, but possibly thought it part of my 'growing-up process'—this was the 'swinging sixties'.

A new lifestyle

Back in Liverpool, only a couple of my friends had not moved on to university or college. A few were still in Chester, but it was too far just to drop in and see them. By this time, I had my own car, a Volkswagen, and, at a loose end, began to drift towards the places of sexual interest I had discovered on my way home from school. While at Blackpool, my voice had broken; I was eighteen at the time and now felt more confident that I was old enough to be sexually attractive to another man. I started meeting people in these sexual cruising places, but still had no sex or even social contact. We would just agree there was nowhere to go for sex and I would disappear. I was still very nervous.

Then, one weekend, my parents had gone away and I had the house to myself. I went out cruising for the evening and met a guy called Hans, who claimed to be German, and took him home. He was about twenty-eight and a rather mysterious character. I found him very attractive indeed. Through Hans I went into a 'gay bar' in Liverpool and ultimately developed a circle of close gay friends and we were very supportive of one another.

I now spent very little time with any of my friends who were not homosexual. Most of them were no longer in the area anyway. The only sense of real duplicity I felt was in my secrecy at home and also at work ...

Within this new circle of friends, there were six of us who were especially close. Some had stable relationships, having been together for many years. They seemed very much to me like married couples. They had set up home together and very rarely went into a gay pub or club. This was to avoid sexual temptation or unfaithfulness ...

Many of the couples that had been together for a long time had an arrangement whereby one partner would be allowed to go off occasionally for another sexual encounter. However, social involvement in these sexual situations was rare, because any emotional attachment would present a threat to the stability of these long-term relationships.

I was fairly promiscuous, although I was, ideally, really longing for a more lasting and stable relationship. With this underlying desire at the back of my mind, sex was something of a hobby. My friends and I frequently shared stories of our sexual encounters. Provided no one was hurt and an existing relationship was not harmed in any way, we had no strong conviction that this way of life was wrong. There was a tremendous sense of loyalty between us. For example, if I became emotionally involved with someone and the relationship did not work out, my friends would contact me to see if I was all right. They would invite me round, or call, to make sure I was coping ...

My social life was therefore quite fulfilling. Mother and father were now much more involved with my friends than ever before. They liked them very much and my friends accepted them in turn. I still had not told my parents about my homosexuality, and although I guessed they probably knew, it still seemed something of a difficult subject to talk about. I wanted to make it clear that my gay lifestyle was different and much more 'normal and acceptable' than my brother's. It was all unspoken, but I assumed they knew most of what was going on in my life and accepted it.

My lifestyle could be compared to some extent with many heterosexuals: enjoying an active sexual life, but always on the look-out for an attractive person who would be a 'good catch'! This, however, was not as apparent as in some parts of the homosexual community, where one can see a real 'rat race' to compete against one another in the 'sexual stakes'. The desire to be attractive can become an all-consuming form of self-idolatry, even though it never really works in the long term. It rarely convinces the person concerned and, in my experience, often drives others away. I guess it is fear and insecurity in one person reacting with similar issues in another. I found the long-lasting homosexual relationships were ones in which the two people involved were different in many ways. They complemented one another, rather than competing or trying to be as physically attractive as each other …

Many of those I met had a deep concern for others and a high standard of 'moral' behaviour, even though I was to learn later that this was not really in accord with Christian standards. For example, if someone was involved in a sexual relationship and did not want to become deeply emotional, he would make that clear to his sexual partner and possibly even break off the relationship. This was so that the other person involved would not get hurt. This was certainly part of my experience. I was nearly always treated with compassion and respect …

It has often been said that the use of the word 'gay' is a lie when referring to homosexuality, but I would have disagreed because in my situation, at that time I would have said there was much gaiety, as in the original meaning of the word. I had developed a lifestyle that was fulfilling and pleasant for me and for my close friends. It was selfish and self-centred in some ways. We did very little to help others, or the world in which we lived, although I must stress that that is far from being the case with other people in the homosexual community. I know many who work very hard for the good of others in self-sacrificing ways.

What reason did I have to believe that my secure little world was not what God wanted for me? None, as far as I could see: I had good friends, a happy social life, a good home and car, plus a secure job. There was one gap in my life that I really longed to be filled. I wanted a lover to whom I was attracted and with whom I could live and share my life. I had already seen something of that with my friends, but somehow it had never really worked out for me. Deep down I realised that I set my standards far too high and was reaching for the impossible, but still that hope lay not too far beneath my consciousness. It was my prayer to a God whom I hoped might be there and bring such a 'knight in shining armour' into my life.

A change of direction

Many of my friends had to give me a heavy push when it came to meeting others socially, with a view to a relationship. I was very shy and found it almost impossible to take the initiative when in a pub or club. One evening, Ken came up to me with a rather shy but nice-looking man. He was not physically tall and overpowering which I normally found attractive, but there was something very pleasant about him. Ken said, 'Martin, I want you to meet Tim.' Then, with a twinkle in his eye, because he knew it would appeal, added, 'Tim is a rugby player.' We started talking and it seemed clear that Ken had met Tim the night before and been to bed with him. Tim did not stay very long, but said he would see me in there again. He seemed very shy and not used to a gay environment ...

The Bonaparte was the name of the club in which I had been introduced to Tim ... One evening at about 9.30 pm, I arrived to find Tim there on his own ... A few weeks before, while living near Preston, he had met another homosexual, also from Liverpool. They had a sexual relationship, but it was the first time Tim had experienced anything like it or met another homosexual socially. He was hurting inside quite a bit. 'I don't really know if this is the sort of life I want,' he said. 'It's all very strange to me.' I tried to assure him that before long it would all seem quite natural and normal ... A couple of nights later he was in the Bonaparte again and I asked him, along with a few others, to come to my place for coffee. He agreed and seemed a bit more willing to talk.

When we were apart from the others in our group, it seemed easier to talk and he told me he had been 'smitten' by this man in Preston ... Then Tim said, 'Martin, I know you will think this sounds silly, but I'm not at all sure that this way of life is right. You see, I am a Christian.' I was quite touched by what I thought was his naivety. I said, 'Well, I'm a Christian too, but I'm sure it's OK. They do say all sorts of leading clergymen are gay and pick up people for sex. I honestly wouldn't worry about that.' I told him of a bishop I'd heard about who picked up men on the M6. Tim didn't seem impressed at all. He was obviously not convinced.

I decided to take him under my wing and show him how much he could enjoy being gay ... I really didn't know whether he was interested in me or not. He was obviously in a very delicate state emotionally and not ready for another relationship just yet. I decided to follow the advice my friends had so often given me before and 'play it cool' with him. I was living in hope, though ...

A few weeks went by with no change in the situation. I was now beginning to feel much more strongly that I wanted a very special relationship with Tim, but for some reason it seemed much more of an emotional desire than a sexual one. I had not made any sexual advances towards him, nor was I burning up with a lust to do so. It may have been because I doubted that Tim was interested in me sexually, although I didn't know for sure that this was true. Eventually I asked him to the theatre for my birthday, and he accepted. The day before our trip I was feeling particularly low and discouraged as far as this new relationship was concerned. I had not really given any thought to Tim's religious beliefs, and in fact he said very little more about them. At about 9 pm I decided to go out for a drink to cheer myself up. Instead of making my usual trip to Liverpool, I went to Chester for a change. At that time the gay bar in Chester was part of a smart hotel in the centre of town. I met a couple of acquaintances there and one guy seemed quite keen for me to go back to his place. I declined his offer and decided to make my own way home alone. While driving down a country road on that chilly March evening I felt a wave of depression hit me. I thought to myself, 'What on earth am I doing with my life? Where's it going?' Thoughts of Tim came into my mind. I was in love once more. I said, 'Oh God, why is all this happening all over again?' Thoughts of unrequited love came to mind ... 'Oh God, not again!'

Immediately a voice within seemed to say, 'Don't worry, Martin. I have brought Tim into your life ... for you!'

I was stunned. 'Was this God speaking—or me?' I felt a strange sense of peace within and real hope. I decided to continue seeking to relate to Tim. I wanted to throw out any doubts that lingered, in case God really had spoken to me. There was a new-found joy in my heart, but after a while another thought suddenly struck me. 'If that really was God, I'd better be good—try to know more about him—otherwise he could change his mind and take Tim away!' I arrived home and went to bed with an instinctive feeling that this was a new beginning in my life.

The next ... afternoon, after work, I decided to make a step towards God and thought I would read the Bible. It was not difficult to find a Bible my uncle had given me when I was christened. It had remained on the bookshelf, almost untouched, for many years. I started to read the Gospel according to St Matthew, which seemed a logical place to begin in the New Testament. I loved my recording of *Jesus Christ Superstar* and had just seen an Italian film, *The Gospel of St Matthew*. I started to read, 'The book of the generation of Jesus Christ, the son of David, the son ...' This really was a new experience for me, but there was something very challenging and exciting about it. In a way the archaic language of the Authorised Version added to the mystique of this new experience. Somehow the words and their sense were not as difficult to understand as I had imagined. There was certainly something very special about the book. I wasn't an avid reader of any books, which made my desire to read my Bible even more surprising.

The next step I decided to take, in trying to please God, was to go to church. This was a mighty and difficult task for me to undertake. I made up my mind to go in the evening, so I would not have to go home for lunch (as I did, nearly every Sunday) afterwards. How could I explain this to my parents, let alone my friends? That evening I put on my best suit and made my way into the little village church, near where I lived. I just hoped that no one would speak to me. I later told Tim I had been to church, but without admitting the difficulties involved in the process. He began to ask if it was a church where the gospel was preached and then explained what he meant by that. He told me how he became a Christian while at school. I often used to hear, in our own school chapel, that Christ died for our sins, though what that actually meant had never been formalised or worked out in my brain. It was just words. As Tim gently shared his own experiences with me, it all made so much more sense than ever before. The idea of sin separating me from God, and Jesus as the perfect sacrifice for that sin, was something I could begin to understand and accept, rather than the complex phraseology of the formal prayers in school. Underlining this new-found understanding of the gospel was the fact that I was beginning to understand something of the perfect humanity of Jesus, through reading Matthew's Gospel. The personality that really shone through the pages to me was one of a perfect man. He seemed to lack any fear, prejudice, anger or other human traits that I had assumed were quite normal. These very special qualities of Jesus made me realise that he really is God and also encouraged me to pay very close attention to all that he was teaching through the Gospel account.

Tim phoned one day to say he had arranged to see a vicar of a church in Wirral, called Roy Barker. 'I have prayed that God will speak to me through him, on this whole question of my homosexuality. Will you pray for me too?' I agreed, with some apprehension. 'How did you get on, Tim?' I asked, when he phoned a couple of hours later. 'Very well. I'm sure our prayers were answered. Roy really seemed to understand what I was talking about. He has come across it before. He said, "Tim, I know some people will tell you differently, but I'm sorry I feel I have to say that Scripture clearly says homosexual practice is wrong. It doesn't condemn you for having a homosexual orientation or temptations."' Tim continued, 'He showed me where this is mentioned in Scripture and I do feel at peace about it now. I am sure he is right, you know. You and I prayed that God would speak through him and I feel that has happened.' 'I'm not sure, Tim,' I said. 'Why should God say it's wrong?' 'Because God intends sex to be only within marriage, between a man and a woman.' 'But why should we have these feelings if they're not right?' I asked. 'I don't know, but I do believe that God can give me the power to overcome them and maybe even take them away. I'd love to be able to get married and have a family, one day.' 'Well, I guess he may be right, but I would have thought if two men loved each other ...' I said, rather unconvinced. 'I really must start going to his church,' Tim said. 'I've heard quite a bit about it. Perhaps you could come over one Sunday?'

I agreed. I knew in my heart that what he was saying was right. Having read Matthew's Gospel I found it difficult to believe that Jesus would condone homosexual relations. It just seemed inconsistent with the rest of his moral teaching. Needless to say, I was a bit reluctant to admit this change of attitude to Tim, because it seemed such an 'about-turn', remembering my efforts to persuade him to accept the homosexual lifestyle! Eventually, at a later meeting, I admitted to him that what Roy had said really did make sense. In my own thinking, the whole idea of loving other people in the way Jesus taught, including other men, gave me something positive and, I thought, potentially fulfilling. It seemed to be an exciting new way of possibly experiencing the love for which I had always craved.

A few weeks later, Tim took me to Upton St Mary's, Roy Barker's church, and I was impressed by so much there. First, it was full. I had no idea that any churches attracted this many people! The general atmosphere was bright and friendly and the order of service was easy to follow ... Even *I* could not feel embarrassed. However, what impressed me more than anything else was the way the people were talking together about what the Lord was doing in their lives.

Roy himself was a stockily built middle-aged man, with slightly thinning dark-brown hair. I was especially struck by his homely nature and gentle fatherly wisdom. His Yorkshire inflection and sense of humour were charming. 'I could probably relate to him, without feeling too daunted or threatened,' I thought.

I managed to see Roy and, like Tim, was struck by his warmth, friendliness and knowledge of 'the subject'. He seemed delighted at what had happened in my life and said, 'Who knows what the Lord has for you to do, Martin? Perhaps even overseas missionary work!'

Confirmation seemed necessary for me to affirm publicly that I had decided to follow Christ. Certainly, my journey to that point had been very unorthodox. All I could say was that God knew my vulnerable emotional needs and used them, and of course Tim, to bring his love into my life.

Jesus told Nicodemus, I tell you the truth, no-one can see the kingdom of God unless he is born again' (John 3:3, NIV). I was beginning to appreciate the reality of that in my own life, as I found so many feelings and attitudes changing. I didn't fully understand the theological meaning of Jesus' words. It just seemed that God was at work in my life, before explaining to me what he was doing.

As I read and understood more Scripture, I found my new faith and experience made a lot of sense. I had a real thirst for God's word, despite the fact that for so many years reading books had not been one of my pastimes. My zeal to learn more helped me to concentrate, although my memory, especially for names, facts and figures, still leaves a lot to be desired! There were times when old insecurities re-surfaced, but I was aware of Jesus' presence in such a real way that they were soon overcome.

As I became more involved in the church in Upton, so Christian fellowship became increasingly important to me. I wanted to share what God was doing in my life and hear more about him through others. There was a wonderful new freedom in not wanting to hide or pretend to be someone I was not.

On the whole I felt pretty good about all that God had been doing in my life, but I had real difficulty identifying or even sympathising with Christians struggling with problems I felt I no longer had. My thinking was that if God could do it for me then he would do it for everyone else. In terms of struggling with temptations and sins, my Christian life seemed to have been pretty smooth sailing. There had been an awareness of my own sinfulness in some areas and of emotional struggles, but there always seemed to be some kind of resolution to them. Sexual temptations had not really been an issue. I regarded this as pretty amazing considering how much my life had revolved around sex since my teenage years. My new way of life as a Christian was so very different from the past that sex didn't seem to be an issue any more. I hadn't masturbated for a couple of years. There were some times of sexual arousal, but the temptation to do anything about it was not really there.

I imagined, without realising it, that God deals with us all in exactly the same way, as if there was some kind of spiritual formula that everyone should experience. I found it difficult to understand why struggling with sexual feelings and desires should really be a problem for committed Christians. Then one day I masturbated! It seemed to happen without a fantasy or desire. It shook me; after a few years as a Christian, how could this happen to me? My emotions had been rocked a bit. My homosexuality, at least the obviously sexual part of it, had resurfaced. Now I found I could identify with many of the people I had possibly even hurt by my lack of real understanding. The words of the Apostle Paul about his 'thorn in the flesh'

(2 Corinthians 12:7) had a whole new meaning for me. I really had been 'elated' in my new-found relationship with Jesus, but judgemental in my attitude to the problems other Christians face. I wouldn't have verbalised it, but Christianity seemed very straightforward to me. I thought you became a Christian and the Holy Spirit enabled you to overcome life's problems and difficulties. The 'honeymoon' period was over for me. I clearly had a lot more to learn about myself, others, and, most importantly, God's ways.

The beginning of a ministry

Roy Barker had a phone call from someone called Geoffrey Percival saying that he believed the person (me) who wrote a letter in *Crusade* (a Christian magazine) went to Roy's church. Geoffrey would be very interested to meet Martin Hallett because of a ministry that he and one or two other people from the Nationwide Festival of Light were about to launch … Geoff was on his way to Poole in Dorset to launch a new ministry to homosexuals to be called Pilot … Many years of experience with Eric Hutchings' evangelistic team had left Geoff with much to share and give, and the ability to communicate the personal application of basic biblical principles clearly and often amusingly.

My brief time with Geoffrey Percival in Poole had not only made me aware of the need for this type of ministry, but it gave me a burning desire to help in some way. As I mulled everything over in my mind and thought of my own experiences, some basic needs emerged that I felt were very important. It seemed to me that it was no good simply counselling people if there was not a church fellowship in which they would be loved, accepted and could grow in Christ. With all my complaints about being lonely, I remembered very clearly how non-judgemental and accepting Christians had been and still were to me. From what Geoff had shared about the fears and reluctance of many churches and individual Christians to face up to the homosexual issue, there seemed a very urgent need for positive teaching … Therefore, I thought the ideal type of ministry would be twofold: partly teaching the Church and partly pastoral support and counselling. I put these ideas down on paper, rather like a job description. I realised that I had created an idea for a workable ministry and wanted to give it some sort of title. [An] event of three years previously, when I had released [a] trapped butterfly, came into mind. Since that time I had seen so many ways in which the 'truth had set me free'.

- Truth in terms of God's love and forgiveness.
- Truth about myself in weakness and strength.
- Truth in terms of honesty and openness with others.

All these and more had set me free in lots of ways, even though of course there was still a long way to go. Therefore the name must somehow encompass truth and freedom. I decided to call my idea 'True Freedom' and believed that God had given me this vision. When I thought of my little bit of counselling experience, the lay ministry and of course what I had been through in terms of my own homosexuality, it seemed that the Lord had been preparing me for all this.

It was decided that I would work from home ... until we had enough funds to pay my salary ... We spent a long time preparing a leaflet and a booklet called *Homosexuality—An Explanation*. All our material would be printed by Upton St Mary's own church press. I prepared the material and gave it to Roy, who then chopped, changed and condensed it. Eventually it was all set up and printed. Advertisements were put in many Christian papers and a letter sent to all local evangelical churches in the area, seeking support. The Trust Deed was signed on 29 June 1977. Once again, a great debt of gratitude was due to Roy for all his loving concern and wisdom. True Freedom Trust was now in operation and we awaited the response.

The original adverts read:

HOMOSEXUALITY
Biblically-based counselling (Harbinger)/teaching (Chandler) ministries,
Free booklet—foolscap sae:
True Freedom Trust, PO Box 8, Liverpool L8 1YL

Initially, many of the people responding to our adverts represented homosexual organisations seeking to find out where we stood. Occasionally there would be one or two strong comments, denouncing us and all we believed. Some clergy argued against us, especially on our stand for scriptural authority. Then there were many more people who wrote expressing appreciation that at last some Christians were taking a stand against homosexuality in the church, but in a personal, pastoral and more positive way. I was not inundated with mail at that time; it was more of a steady trickle. I kept thinking that the Lord must have a strange sense of humour, giving me a ministry which consisted mainly of writing letters to people. This had always been quite an ordeal. I was so self-conscious about my layout and grammar, wondering what people might think of me. The most difficult letters of course were the replies to people struggling with homosexual problems. They were nearly all Christians. Some had never shared their difficulties with anyone else before ...

Most people contacting us, having not shared their difficulties with other Christians, are fairly convinced they will be misunderstood and rejected. Such rejection may not be in terms of a positive decision or verbalised statement. It is more likely to be a much more subtle rejection, often not recognised as such by the person guilty of it. Even today, I find myself at fault in this area in regard to my attitude to my old gay friends. Because I find I cannot identify with them and sometimes even feel uncomfortable in their company for many different reasons, I avoid the situation and make few steps towards them. I may not want to admit that I have rejected them, but in fact I have done just that.

Some of the people contacting me live a kind of double existence; on the one hand being involved with Christian fellowship, but then slipping into homosexual activity compulsively—usually the anonymous type of one-off sexual encounters, experiencing a sudden giving in to temptation, followed, of course, by tremendous guilt. Pornography is a big problem for many Christians, including those with no experience of homosexual relationships, the Internet now being a major source. It is a private world and a seemingly intimate one of fascination and excitement. Of course it isn't really as private as one hopes. Pornography soon becomes an addiction, once sexual pleasure has been gained from it. Before the World Wide Web almost every magazine stand could be a fascination and cause real temptation. Homosexual pornography was not as readily available as its heterosexual counterpart, but in some ways that made the search for it a compulsive, soul-destroying drive. Again and again the same story would be told: 'I pick up the pornography, use it perhaps once or twice, feel disgusted with myself and destroy it. Then I find myself in the shop again ...' Such excitement has now become much more accessible through the computer. Gay chatrooms and porn of every conceivable type are available online.

Early in 1979, I read a book from America by two Christian women from an evangelical background. Neither was apparently homosexual. They came down on the side of supporting homosexual relationships in certain situations. Many of their arguments were not new to me. They were basically echoing what the more 'liberal' theologians were saying, but it was dressed up in more evangelical terminology. The two main points which impressed me were their arguments against the hurt and prejudice shown by many Christians and churches (having seen something of this), and the fact that they were not homosexual themselves and therefore seemingly unbiased.

Needless to say, reading this book left me very unsettled and insecure. I was not convinced they were right, but still wondered if I could be wrong. Up to this point I tended to accept much of what I was reading on the subject of homosexuality, because I agreed and could understand the strong biblical basis on which it was all founded. Perhaps I had not really thought it all through thoroughly for myself. But now I felt lonely and frightened. Over these few days I was forced into doing a lot of thinking and praying. Eventually I felt more positive and secure in my beliefs. This had been a painful but necessary experience. It helped me to see how easily convinced someone with strong homosexual feelings could be by the arguments of a more liberal theology, when expressed by a Christian claiming to believe in the authority of Scripture. Understanding what God is saying to us today, through his word the Bible, is a lifelong process. I remember meeting a well-known Bible teacher, a retired bishop, who said, 'It never ceases to amaze me how much more I have to learn about the wonders of God's Word!' I replied, 'Wow, if you think that, where does it leave the likes of me!' So, yes, I'm still learning, especially in the area of the Bible and sexuality.

It now seems to me that the only possible way to claim that God does not condemn all sex between same-sex partners, is to say that the scriptures concerned are not God's Word to me today. But to do this would undermine the very foundations of my faith and the truth of the gospel of Christ.

Hope and healing?

Over the years some have suggested I am not open enough to a change in sexual orientation. They may be right. Maybe they have found in their own lives the ability to love and be fulfilled heterosexually, when previously homosexuality seemed to be their only sexual option. Some have even said to me that only the hope of a real heterosexual relationship keeps them going on with God. It has been argued, from Genesis 2, that heterosexuality is God's ideal, and therefore what we should all be aiming to experience. Should we really all desire heterosexual feelings if we are not married? Is the heterosexuality we see in Genesis not very different from what we now define as heterosexuality? It seems likely to me that, before the Fall, there was only sexual attraction and desire within that one relationship and certainly a complete absence of embarrassment, shame and guilt. This is a sexual purity that none of us will entirely experience in this world—in the same way that none of us will experience a freedom from ageing and weariness because of the Fall. How much of our 'pre-fallen state' can and should we really seek or expect to experience this side of eternity? There won't be any sexual problems in heaven, for sure. Perhaps there won't even be any sex. We certainly won't be worried about it!

When I look back at what God has done in my life over my thirty years as a Christian, it is amazing. I must admit I have probably not reminded myself of this often enough. Perhaps I am guilty of accepting it to the point of taking it for granted. For sure, there have been many times when God's presence and power have been there dramatically, but more often it has been as 'my storyteller'—that is, an awareness of God in all that goes on, teaching, leading, comforting and empowering.

The problem we all face when addressing the issue of hope and healing is a very big one—ourselves! Our own desires, fears, self-aspirations and hopes are influenced and therefore to some extent driven by our imperfect humanity. In other words, our attitude towards the issue of our 'fallen humanity' and its healing is probably as corrupted by the Fall as the issue itself. When looking at what we mean by healing and hope, we are inevitably limited by our humanity. I believe that because we are unable to fully understand God's definition of healing, we try to make it conform to human logic and understanding, which is radically different. Although we say, 'God's ways are not our ways' I doubt we really accept the full extent of that statement.

I believe we must start by appreciating that throughout history God's desire has been to communicate his love to his creation. Clearly this is expressed in a multitude of ways. One of them must be the expression of his love to humankind. In other words, God's desire is for us to know we are loved and valued by him. This process of communication between the Creator and ourselves has been fulfilled through God's forgiveness and redemption in the Lord Jesus. This seems to me the main biblical definition of hope. It is all to do with our relationship with ourselves (i.e. self-worth) and the Creator, partly experienced here and now, but only perfected in glory. The process of growth towards this ultimate healing must involve knowing we are valuable as God's creation and learning to receive God's love and forgiveness.

It sounds so obvious, but this is something we can find painfully difficult to really experience. Yet it is the healing life-blood for most of our emotional problems. In the mid-1980s, I believed my major problem was loneliness and I thought God simply wanted to meet that need through Christian relationships, empowered by the Holy Spirit. I now realise that loneliness is usually much more than a legitimate need for other people. Right at the core or centre of our sense of 'being' there is often a feeling of emptiness—'Who am I?' ... 'Where do I belong?' ... 'To whom do I belong?' I guess in a sense it is a God-created human need. It is linked to our sense of worth and value, not just to a person, but to the world in which we live. I used to quote the famous words of Genesis, where God tells us we are not meant to be alone, seeing that simply as our God-created need for human relationships. This is quite correct, of course, but not the whole story. It seems to me that when God said this to the man it was before the Fall, when man's relationship with God was perfect. This means, even when we have a 'perfect' relationship with God, we still need other people. The problem is, we do not now have a perfect relationship with God and even ourselves, through low self-worth. In other words, we are hindered in our loving because we do not fully believe we are lovable. We are not finding our fundamental or core sense of value through the love of God for us. I wonder if it is this sense of loneliness, often unrecognised, which drives our demand for human relationships. We think they will satisfy this deeply rooted sense of value and identity, and at times in the highs of loving relationships they do seem to work. However, ultimately they often don't, and we return to the emptiness, maybe deciding to try once again to find another lover.

So often I, and many other Christians, have majored much on the therapeutic value of relationships. It was what we wanted to hear ... 'You can have affectionate, loving relationships, but make sure you don't have sex!' Personally, I find it very difficult to just have affectionate relationships when there's a mutual sexual attraction. Sexual temptation is very difficult to resist. I can idealistically talk about my love for the other person not wanting to encourage us to sin, but my body can go into 'overdrive' and sexual feelings can take control. The point I am trying to make is that this search for a perfect human relationship is not the real answer for loneliness. I can only fulfil my God-created need for relationships with others when my relationship with myself, through God's love, is good and secure. One of my gripes in today's culture are those convenient, but I think often anti-social, mobile phones. Maybe it's my own prejudices, but I wonder if the incessant text messaging is sometimes a symptom of this inner loneliness I've tried to describe. (I'm hopeless at text messaging anyway!)

We can, however, work at overcoming the hurts and fears that hinder and obstruct this process of believing and receiving the perfect love of God. As I keep saying, one barrier is likely to be a low self-image, of which homosexual desires may be but one example in our lives. I don't mean simply in terms of our attitude towards our homosexuality, but the low self-worth from which it has evolved and which now drives our homosexual desires.

If we are at work in this process of a growing sense of our self-worth and value, through receiving God's love, this will involve learning to value everything in our lives, good and bad, including our sexuality. In other words, we need to believe that our life story is valuable. If we do, we are more likely to believe we are valuable ourselves. God is the storyteller, who allows everything to happen in our lives. This can be a scary idea, when we view it through the tainted lenses of our 'logical' fallen humanity. 'Why does a God of love and goodness allow evil, suffering and sin?' We cannot hope to fully answer that question. Our human brains are not programmed to do so. We 'see in a mirror dimly' in this life. But we can at least learn to accept it, and I wonder if doing so is also an important part of the 'healing' process.

As we begin to experience the truth of our personal value, and the value of all life's experiences, we may find that our sexuality changes, as do many other feelings. We are dealing with some of the low self-worth components in our personal development. However, inevitably, it is unlikely to be quite that predictable, because sometimes God's means of showing his love and forgiveness involves allowing us to experience problems and sin. This is not humanly logical, but part of the mystery of God's ways. How can we know grace, unless our experience of sin encourages us to seek it? 'The law was added so that the trespass might increase. But where sin increased, grace increased all the more, so that, just as sin reigned in death, so also grace might reign through righteousness to bring eternal life through Jesus Christ our Lord. What shall we say, then? Shall we go on sinning, so that grace may increase? By no means! We died to sin; how can we live in it any longer?' (Romans 5:20–6:2, NIV).

I am not trying to say that God wants us to sin so that we will know more of his love and forgiveness. God hates sin and of course cannot have anything to do with it. But perhaps we are not good at dealing with sin because we are not good at receiving God's forgiveness ... I guess I find, as do many others, there is usually a slippery slope towards sin. I can easily try to convince myself that I can't help it. The truth is, I always have a choice not to sin. I know if I start titillating my desires, for example as I browse the

Internet, it can easily lead to further problems and sin. I have choices to make before that starts, and if I do make the right choices there is a sense of freedom that is liberating. I also need to delete the results of my sinful roamings, not simply to hide the evidence, but as an act of repentance and worship. That may have to be an ongoing process and it must never stop. The sense of cleansing and freedom may be, for some of us, enough to prevent the problem occurring, but we must never be complacent. Our lives as Christians will be a continuing healing process of dealing with sins, and therefore receiving God's love and forgiveness.

We are also reminded through Job and the Apostle Paul in 2 Corinthians 12:7–8 that Satan is ultimately under God's authority as a created being: 'To keep me from being conceited because of these surpassingly great revelations, there was given me a thorn in my flesh, a messenger of Satan, to torment me. Three times I pleaded with the Lord to take it away from me' (NIV). Satan only has as much 'rope' as God allows him to have. But why does God allow Satan to do anything? Why not simply destroy him now and give us all some peace? Well, Paul, Job and we also, need to learn, grow and ultimately know more of God's love and goodness, through evils that are allowed in our lives. So we sometimes seem to be dealing with paradoxes, in the sense of our human understanding. God hates evil and sin, but allows it. God is in control of all, but nevertheless wants us to fight for goodness and overcome evil. He often gives us the strength to do so, but sometimes does not, otherwise we would not struggle and fail as we do. God knew when he created us with a free will that we would disobey him and he would need to die in order to redeem our sin. What sense does any of that make in our so-called human logic where we want answers to everything!

We can stop struggling to understand the incomprehensible and learn to accept it. We can work with this apparent paradox and see its value. When we value stories of people like Job, we can value our own stories, which will involve the same dynamics. Although our own stories may not be as dramatic, they are just as valuable to ourselves and to others. In this way, we learn to work with the good and the bad, seeing it all redeemed. That does not mean that we stop fighting against sin, in all its forms—both in us and in society. But we learn to know more of God's love and forgiveness. We see the truth that 'in all things God works for the good of those who love him' (Romans 8:28, NIV). The good is for us, for others and for God's kingdom.

How can my sexual desires and sin ultimately work for this 'good'? It may be in several ways, uniquely for each person. For example, my desires may be saying I am feeling unloved and not affirmed. What am I going to do about that, through my relationship with God, myself and others? My sexual habit or addiction may be indicating or feeding on my state of loneliness, boredom or even tiredness. What am I going to do about that, through my lifestyle? Maybe I am experiencing a 'thorn' as a sin because I have been too judgemental in my attitudes to others who are struggling? Perhaps I am a 'Job's comforter'? Perhaps I have not really understood the struggles of another, but now … 'Wow, now I know how they felt!'

All these have been a part of my experience and I guess will continue to be so. I have at times struggled with issues, including sexual ones, which I thought were either dead or buried or would never be a part of my experience. I'm not proud of that, but the experience has been and will continue to be part of my ministry, and in that sense I can value them. I can therefore understand those who struggle with addictive sexual behaviour, including cruising, phone lines and the Internet. I appreciate the importance of accountability and identifying the underlying problems. My ministry has been a great source of healing for me, as I've listened to and shared with others, often thereby seeing the value of my own story. Frequently, when I felt unworthy to help others, my ministry hasn't given me an opportunity to opt out. I have then seen God's ordaining of a ministry situation, because of my own problems, not despite them. In other words, I have realised that my own experience has helped another, maybe through understanding, maybe because I have found (or am finding) a way through for myself. Sometimes all or none of those situations were involved, yet I have been used. I could see it as a way in which God has certainly shown his love for me, and hopefully I have been able to express that to someone else. If that is true in my ministry, it must be true in yours. After all, we all have a ministry, whatever our life experiences, abilities or disabilities may be.

When we become Christians, it is said to be vital that we share what has happened with someone else. Witnessing to the truth in this way gives it a kind of root and stability in our own lives, as well as hopefully encouraging others. I passionately believe this is not only true for the time of our conversion. It is just as important for us to share our story with others as it goes on. Clearly it may be necessary to share some things as principles, rather than all the specific details. I often suggest to church leaders how important it is for them to share their sexuality struggles as part of their teaching and preaching. Following the look of shock and horror on their faces, I qualify that by saying it can be shared as a struggle with sin and brokenness. The Apostle Paul talked about his struggle with sin and 'doing what he did not want to do, rather than what he knew he should be doing'. He didn't tell us exactly what sins he was struggling with, but he knew the full details. He was therefore being honest and sharing the truth. He would not have felt, as many leaders I meet, a sense of dishonesty and hypocrisy. I guess even sharing in terms of euphemisms can seem a bit scary, but it need not be so. It is therapeutic, because in sharing what we are learning of the truth of God's love and of ourselves, we are also more likely to be confirming those truths for ourselves. In this way a theological truth moves from being an idea to a feeling, and then to a personal experience.

I believe this process of learning about love is also learning to love. This is healing based on the real hope we see expressed within the Bible. Rarely, if ever, in Scripture are we given directly a hope of what God is going to do for us. Hope is nearly always expressed in terms of what God has done for us at the cross and in terms of our redemption.

I believe we make a big mistake when we base a ministry mainly on the hope of what God may do for us in the here and now. In doing so we appeal to the perfectionist in us and may well be encouraging at some point a sense of failure, possibly resulting in a rejection of Christianity or the adoption of a more liberal approach to it. Perhaps we are even unwittingly aiding the accuser and deceiver, who may be saying, 'This is what God will do for you!' knowing only too well that if it doesn't happen, God will be rejected. Over the years, I have seen the tragedy of so many Christians giving up on God because of what they see as their unfulfilled expectations and hopes. We must seek never to be guilty of encouraging this in any way. 'If in this life only we have hoped in Christ, we are of all people most to be pitied' (1 Corinthians 15:9).

What about the church?

If you ask the average gay or lesbian person what they believe evangelical Christians think of them, they will say, 'They hate us, don't they? They hate homosexuals!' This is the message they have often received because of campaigns against homosexuality by Christians. We may say, 'we love the sinner but hate the sin'; however, an unbeliever will rarely be able to make that distinction. We also need to appreciate that many homosexuals have really struggled to find self-acceptance and have often been on the receiving end of prejudice. They have developed a morality based on two people loving one another and being faithful. They will find it difficult, if not impossible, to understand why that should be wrong, especially when no one is harmed and the people concerned feel loved, affirmed and secure in their relationship. A Christian condemnation of this will therefore feel offensive and abusive, possibly even cruel. This will be especially true if the road the person has travelled to reach this point of fulfilment has been a difficult one. In a sense a Christian condemnation of this person's moral choices will actually 'offend his or her morality'.

We may also find that young evangelical Christians have a similar reaction to the traditional evangelical view of homosexuality. They may have gay and lesbian friends whom they like and they may possibly admire the quality of their relationships. They will assume their more traditional evangelical brethren simply don't understand the issue of homosexuality, because of comments that they hear.

This means we must not rely on a theology that condemns homosexuality because it doesn't bring happiness and fulfilment. This is flawed reasoning and will encourage disillusionment when people meet happy and fulfilled homosexuals. I believe homosexual sex offends God because it is not what he originally intended sex to be. It is not simply in terms of the correct functioning of male and female genitalia, but in the 'divine mystery of one flesh'. Perhaps, originally God intended the sexual act to be an act of worship, celebrating the very act of his creation—woman from man—reunited as one flesh. The concept of any sex outside this 'male with female' ideal offending God, is the only reasoning that makes sense to me.

We also need to realise that our legitimate needs to know love and fulfilment with others should be met within the body of Christ. This is often difficult, especially for single people, including homosexuals, who feel unpartnered and lonely. Finding emotional fulfilment outside the church can be very tempting.

I am really grateful to God for my sexuality, even though it has been both a problem and a blessing. It has enabled me to love and understand myself and others, both within close relationships and in the wider ministry of the church. Most importantly, it has been a major catalyst to my understanding and receiving of God's love. It has helped me in learning to know love—the truth which sets me free. Is that your experience? It certainly can be if you choose to learn God's way of loving. If my story has been of any help at all, so will yours.

Martin Hallett's book *Still Learning to Love* (HOW Publications, 2004), as well as information about the work of True *f*reedom Trust and details of other ministries worldwide, can be obtained from:

T*f*T
PO Box 13
Prenton
Wirral
UK
CH43 6YB
Tel: +44 (0) 151 653 0773
Info@truefreedomtrust.co.uk
www.truefreedomtrust.co.uk